EFFECTIVE TELEPHONE SKILLS

Second Edition

Thomas J. Farrell

Johnson & Wales University

The Dryden Press
Harcourt Brace College Publishers

Fort Worth Philadelphia San Diego New York Orlando Austin San Antonio Toronto
Montreal London Sydney Tokyo

Acquisitions Editor	Emily Thompson
Art Director	Pat Bracken
Production Manager	Ann Coburn
Photo & Permissions Editor	Elizabeth Banks
Marketing Manager	Shelly Hoger
Editorial Assistant	Tracy Morse
Electronic Publishing Coordinator	Jill Stubblefield
Electronic Publishing Manager	Michael Beaupré
Director of Editing, Design, & Production	Diane Southworth
Publisher	Elizabeth Widdicombe
Text Type	10/12 Galliard
Cover Art	Yves Courbet

PHOTOCREDITS:

p. 4   © 1990 J. P. H. Images/The Image Bank
p. 5   © David Ximeno Tejada/Tony Stone Images
p. 8   © Dennis MacDonald/PhotoEdit
p. 18 © Bruce Ayres/Tony Stone Images
p. 20 © Walter Bibikow/The Image Bank
p. 28 © Rohan/Tony Stone Images
p. 29 © David Young-Wolff/PhotoEdit
p. 34 © Gregory Heisler/The Image Bank
p. 35 © Schmid/Langsfeld/The Image Bank
p. 42 © David Young-Wolff/PhotoEdit
p. 44 © James L. Shaffer
p. 77 © Primero Productions R/The Image Bank
p. 82 © David Young-Wolff/PhotoEdit
p. 84 © Paul Conklin/PhotoEdit
p. 86 © Tim Brown/Tony Stone Images
p. 87 © Robert Brenner/PhotoEdit

Requests for permission to make copies of any part of the work should be mailed to: Permissions Department, Harcourt Brace & Company, Orlando, FL 32887.

Address for Editorial Correspondence
The Dryden Press, 301 Commerce Street, Suite 3700, Fort Worth, TX 76102

Address for Orders
The Dryden Press, 6277 Sea Harbor Drive, Orlando, FL 32887
1-800-782-4479 or 1-800-433-0001 (in Florida)

ISBN: 0-03-098343-6

Library of Congress Catalog Card Number: 94-70436

Printed in the United States of America

4 5 6 7 8 9 0 1 2 3   023   9 8 7 6 5 4 3 2 1

The Dryden Press
Harcourt Brace College Publishers

Preface

The second edition of *Effective Telephone Skills* combines the successful features of the first edition with new materials that reflect recent technological developments in business telephone communications.

This book is built on two basic premises:

1. The telephone is a primary communications link in today's business world.
2. In order to be successful, individuals must be able to communicate effectively by telephone.

These premises are reflected in the organization of the book into two major sections. Part 1, "Fundamentals of Telephone Communication," explains concepts and theories necessary to understanding the telephone as a vital communications tool. Part 2, "Sharpening Your Telephone Skills," contains realistic simulations of telephone situations that give students the opportunity not only to learn effective techniques but to practice them as well. It is through this combination of theory and real-world exercises that students will develop the skills needed for success.

The structuring of simulation exercises in the classroom will depend, to some extent, on whether or not telephone equipment is available. If equipment is available, it can add realism to the exercise. But if equipment is not available, simulated exercises can, with the use of a little imagination, be quite effective. What is important, of course, is that students be given the chance to react "live" to another party in a specific situation. In a given exercise, the instructor may play the role of the "other party" or may assign the role to members of the class.

Each chapter begins with Learning Objectives that spell out for the students what they should be able to do at the conclusion of the chapter. Assignments are provided, which can be done either in or out of class, and quizzes test the major points made in each chapter. Finally, the Appendix contains additional exercises and an answer key to the review quizzes.

To the Student: If you plan to be a switchboard operator/receptionist, secretary, administrative assistant, or telemarketer, this book will help you achieve your goal. If, however, your objective is another type of business career, you will find that this book offers you a broader understanding of the role of the telephone in achieving good communication in business. Regardless, then, of your specific plans for the future, you should find the insights and exercises in this book valuable. Finally, relax, enjoy yourself, and remember that it is quite possible to learn and have fun at the same time.

Acknowledgments: I would like to thank my assistants, Monique Blouin and Susan Jones, for their assistance in preparing the manuscript. I would also like to thank those who were kind enough to read the manuscript and make suggestions: Louise St. Cyr of Katherine Gibbs, Patricia Mason-Browne of the University of Iowa, Teresa Ferguson of the ITT Technical Institute, Diane Monica, and Joan Ryan.

Thomas J. Farrell

Table of Contents

v

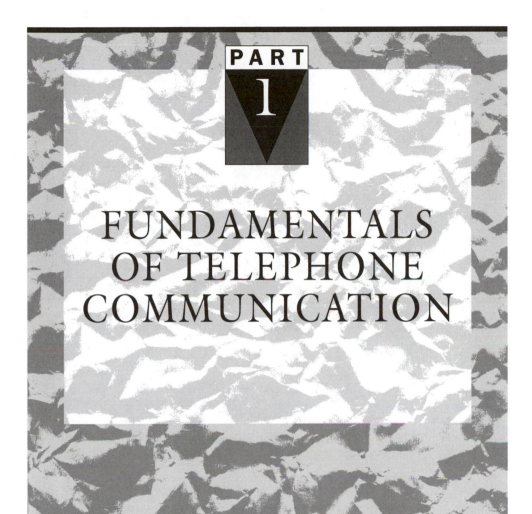

PART 1

FUNDAMENTALS OF TELEPHONE COMMUNICATION

Increasing Your Telephone Awareness

Learning Objectives

At the completion of this chapter, you will be able to

■ Explain why telephone skills are of such importance to businesses in an information economy.

■ Define the term *public relations* and explain why the telephone is a public relations tool.

■ Identify personality traits that are ideal for effective telephone skills.

■ Recognize personality traits that may make the acquiring of telephone skills a more difficult task.

■ Describe specific behaviors that represent your present telephone personality.

1.1 A NEW FOCUS ON TELEPHONE SKILLS

Recently a major corporation that operates a large chain of business education schools surveyed 450 companies in cities around the country. The purpose of the survey was to learn what skills corporate leaders thought were most important for new and existing employees to have. The results of the survey were used to design an innovative curriculum program, one that would prepare students for a rapidly changing business environment. Some of the responses were predictable, reflecting the advance of modern technology such as the ability to use word processors and computers. What some people might find surprising, however, was that among all the space-age skills listed the third most desired group of skills was plain, old-fashioned telephone skills!

Telephone skills, you say? What's a dowdy 118-year-old invention doing on the same list with all those newfangled machines? Alexander Graham Bell's famous words to his assistant, "Mr. Watson, come here. I want you,"—spoken on March 10, 1876, are ancient history today. The telephone is no longer considered to be as miraculous an invention as it once was. There are many more impressive devices such as television, video recorders, and fax machines that are commonplace now so the telephone is taken for granted. That, of course, might just be the problem.

The reason you take the telephone for granted is that, from the time you were very young, it was part of the standard furnishings in your homes, not much different from tables, sofas, and chairs. As toddlers, you played

Our first telephone conversations are usually casual, informal transactions.

with toy telephones and had your first live conversations on telephones with relatives who were away from home. As you grew older, the telephone was a connection to your developing circle of friends and, when you became a teenager, it became both the means to carry on youthful romances and a source of conflict as your parents tried to keep the lines free for more important matters. Occasionally, you panicked when it had to be used to arrange prom dates or other such traumatic events but, more often than not, it was a comfortable way to carry on casual conversation.

So why the big fuss about something you have been doing for most of your lives? The answer to that question lies in the different purposes of telephones in today's business world. *Most business telephone conversations are formal transactions engaged in for specific purposes, and they require a different set of behaviors than are used in our personal informal telephone usage.* To help you understand the increased importance of the telephone as a means of business communication, it is necessary to look at the broader changes that have occurred in recent years.

1.2   THE TELEPHONE IN THE INFORMATION ECONOMY

Since the early 1980s social scientists have been heralding the transition in our society from an industrial economy to an **information economy.** Simply put, this means that many more Americans work at jobs whose purpose is to provide or produce information than work at goods-producing jobs such as manufacturing or agriculture. The list of information jobs is endless, beginning with the obvious ones such as clerks, librarians, systems

There is a new sense of urgency and importance about telephone usage.

analysts, and is growing to include occupations in computer manufacturing, telecommunications, printing, mass media, advertising, accounting, education, finance, insurance, and positions as information workers employed in noninformation firms. Some of the nation's major corporations, such as AT&T, IBM, XEROX, and ITT, are information companies who employ hundreds of thousands of workers.

John Naisbitt, author and futurist, saw the relationship between the new information economy and communications technology this way:

> The life channel of the information age is communication. In simple terms, communication requires a sender, a receiver, and a communication channel. The introduction of increasingly sophisticated information technology has revolutionized that simple process. The net effect is a faster flow of information through the information channel, bringing sender and receiver closer together, or collapsing the **information float**—the amount of time information spends in the communication channel.

What Naisbitt called the "collapsing of the information float" has created an interesting phenomenon. Living in a fast-paced world in which computers and television provide instantaneous access to data and news, we are no longer willing to wait for information. People in today's society have become accustomed to the immediate, the here and now, and we are uncomfortable with delays of any kind. Family phone bills have escalated as relatives and friends abandon the custom of letter writing and, in its place, substitute the long-distance phone call. As usual, technology has changed our **behaviors** and our **attitudes**—how we act and how we think.

In business, the impact of this "collapse of the information float" is clear. With instant information available to us, we are impatient to communicate our messages and unwilling to put up with the week-and-a-half "float" needed for the conventional exchange of written business correspondence. There is a new sense of urgency and importance about telephone usage. Some affluent golfers, for instance, have equipped their golf carts with phones so they can transact business between shots. While phones on golf carts are not standard equipment for most of us, certainly beepers and car phones are becoming commonplace. Many business people believe that, regardless of where they are, they must be able to be in touch should the situation warrant it.

Although detailed complex issues are still better handled by written correspondence, the trend toward increased telephone usage is definite. This tendency is not limited to our own country. By the end of this decade, the world will have one billion telephones, all of them interconnected and almost all capable of dialing direct to any other. Indeed, many of the business transactions in the global village of the future will be conducted by telephone.

1.3   TELEPHONE TRAINING

Because of this changed environment corporate executives and managers are insisting that their employees understand that the telephone is a business tool they must learn to use well. To ensure this, companies are turning to specialists to get the job done. George Walther and Nancy Friedman are two such specialists.

George Walther, the author of *Phone Power—How to Make the Telephone Your Most Profitable Business Tool,* earns his living providing telephone technique training and consulting to corporations ranging from Control Data, Citicorp, and Xerox to small businesses and nonprofit organizations. Even the U.S. Senate and Department of Commerce have hired him to improve their staffs' phone skills. Walther is able to get his clients' attention and their business by citing the following facts:

1. There is no single activity American business people spend more time doing (and less time improving) than using the telephone. Upper-level managers spend twice as much time phoning as they spend doing paperwork or reading . . . scheduled meetings account for 31 percent less time than phone calls . . . . Executives spend two-and-a-half times as many hours handling phone calls as handling mail.
2. The only business tools used more intensively than the phone are pen or pencil and paper. As a business ally, a tool that should help us get much more accomplished, the telephone is sorely undervalued.

That lack of respect for the telephone is changing fast. No one understands this change in corporate values and behavior more clearly than Nancy Friedman, the "Telephone Doctor," who claims her satisfied clients include United Van Lines, Union Carbide, Goodyear, and Digital Equipment. Ms. Friedman's "doctoring" is not inexpensive. She charges $2500 for four-hour, in-house training sessions and gets it! The dollar amount ($2500) is significant, because it is proof of the importance that corporate decision makers place on effective telephone usage. Ms. Friedman argues that every member of an organization, from the president to the maintenance person, should be a skilled phone user.

What meaning do the George Walther and Nancy Friedman stories have for young men and women looking ahead to successful careers? The answer to that question should be obvious. Major corporations, such as those you hope to work for, realize how valuable telephone skills are. You should, too. If you are not convinced yet, pay attention to the advice of Stanley Bing who in a satirical article titled "The Strategist" in *Esquire* magazine stated:

> Aside from the credit card, the telephone is the ultimate business tool. It eliminates the need for meetings with unnecessary people, enables you to pollinate myriad flowers, while brown-bagging it at your desk, and slices odious paper flow. As with any instrument, mastery takes talent, practice.

If you wish to be successful in your business career, do yourself a favor. Resolve now to become a talented telephone user.

1.4   THE TELEPHONE AS A PUBLIC RELATIONS TOOL

Before there can be a change in behavior, there must first be a change in attitude. You must change the way you think and feel about the telephone. Put aside the attitudes you acquired about telephone use while you were growing up at home. Instead, substitute a new set of ideas which suggest that every time you use the telephone in business, you are a public relations representative of the company that employs you. As such, you have the opportunity to create **goodwill** for your employer. Many people with whom you speak will form their impressions of your company, its products, and services, by the way you present yourself to them on the phone. For some customers, their only contact with your company may be by telephone. It makes little difference whether you are in an entry-level position or are a senior executive. To the person you are talking to, you *are* the company. Along with the potential to create a positive image comes the opposite possibility. Consider this actual example of both positive and negative public relations within the same company.

After seeing a family of five children through college, a colleague of mine and his wife made plans to visit London for a week. It was their first trip out of the country, and they were understandably excited. They booked a tour through a major airline, sent off a deposit, and expected to be billed for the balance of the cost a month or so before departure. When neither bill nor tickets arrived as expected, the husband called the airline one morning to resolve the problem. The first representative he spoke with told my friend he had made an error, the trip would now be more expensive than quoted, and when a disagreement ensued, ended the conversation by hanging up! After waiting until his anger subsided, my colleague called the airline once again that afternoon. To his surprise and delight, the second airline representative listened sympathetically to his problem, apologized on behalf of the airline for the earlier offense, arranged for the transaction to be completed at the original price, and did all of this with warmth and courtesy. The story is useful to us, because it illustrates how employees of the same company can be either public relations liabilities or assets.

Today, as American businesses strive to operate successfully in a very competitive world market, corporations are searching for better ways to

Every time you use the telephone in business, you are a public relations representative of the company that employs you.

gain and keep new customers. As so often is the case, this search has come full circle, back to the basics of providing quality products and good service. One of the speakers who carries that message in his lectures is Thomas J. Peters, author, lecturer, and business consultant. Peters is in such great demand because his formula for corporate success can be implemented at low cost if employees are willing to do what it takes to get the job done. Peters states, "The excellent companies really are close to their customers." The telephone is the primary way that most companies maintain contact with their customers. It is the means by which they provide service, generate goodwill, and sustain long-term, mutually profitable business relationships. The remainder of this book is devoted to helping you develop the telephone skills that you will need if you are to play your part in your employer's quest for excellence.

1.5   YOUR TELEPHONE PERSONALITY

If you are convinced about the importance of good telephone technique in business, it is time to take the next step. To accomplish your objective of becoming proficient at telephone use, you must first take stock of your present telephone personality. This "taking stock" or self-inventory should identify those things you do well and not so well. First, you need to assess your own personality to see how it affects your current telephone communication. When this straightforward assessment is completed, you will be ready to begin a change in attitude and behavior that will improve your skills.

Each time you pick up the phone to call someone or to answer a call, you bring to that communication your own unique **personality**. It is unlike anyone else's. Your personality has been in the process of becoming since you were born (perhaps before) and is the product of both biological and environmental influences. We are not so much concerned here with how you became the person you are, but that you be aware of the nature of your own personality and how it may affect your telephone behavior. Take a few minutes to answer the following questions about your personality as you think it is now. Compare your answers to the "ideal" answers that follow; then move on and take the Telephone Personality Test.

Insights into Personality

Circle Yes or No.

1.	Do you think of yourself as an introvert?	YES	NO
2.	Do you usually allow others to do the talking because you are reluctant to speak?	YES	NO
3.	Do you think other people generally have better ideas to offer than you?	YES	NO
4.	Do you think of yourself as an extrovert?	YES	NO
5.	Do you seek out the company of friends?	YES	NO
6.	Do you encourage dialogue with others and are you receptive to other points of view?	YES	NO
7.	Do you offer new ideas willingly?	YES	NO

8. Do you dominate conversations?	YES	NO
9. Do you feel your own ideas are best?	YES	NO
10. Do you enjoy persuading others to accept your ideas?	YES	NO
11. Do you think of yourself as having healthy self-confidence?	YES	NO
12. Do you enjoy meeting and talking with strangers?	YES	NO
13. Do you consider yourself to be a good listener?	YES	NO
14. Do you consider yourself a courteous person?	YES	NO
15. Do you consider yourself to be a well-organized individual?	YES	NO

The following pattern of answers suggests an individual who has a personality that is ideal for effective telephone use:

1. No	**6.** Yes	**11.** Yes
2. No	**7.** Yes	**12.** Yes
3. No	**8.** No	**13.** Yes
4. Yes	**9.** No	**14.** Yes
5. Yes	**10.** Yes	**15.** Yes

To the extent that your answers differ from the ideal pattern, you will have to work harder at developing your skills. Consider that a challenge and remember that, while it is true that our basic personalities are formed during early childhood, it is never too late for us, as adults, to change overt behaviors and acquire new skills.

1.6   TELEPHONE PERSONALITY TEST—A PERSONAL ASSESSMENT

It is time to move from a general consideration of your personality and the possibility of change to a more specific focus on your telephone personality. Evidence from research supports the conclusion that the most successful people are those who know themselves and know the demands of a particular skill and adopt strategies to meet those demands. To help you do this, take a few minutes to take the diagnostic test that follows. This test will give you a better understanding of your present telephone habits. Please remember that there are no right or wrong answers. Answer the questions honestly, keeping in mind that the first answer that occurs to you is likely to be the most accurate.

Circle the answer that best describes your present telephone behavior. If you have already worked in an office, base your answers on that experience. If not, use your telephone habits at home as your reference or base them on the way you feel you would act in business situations without prior training.

1. Before placing an important call, I jot down the points I wish to discuss in the order I wish to discuss them.

   Always   *Sometimes*   *Seldom*

2. I Identify myself immediately at the beginning of a conversation whether placing or receiving a call.

   Always   *Sometimes*   *Seldom*

3. When placing a call, I ask whether the other party has time to take my call.

   Always   *Sometimes*   *Seldom*

4. I dial long-distance calls direct whenever possible.

   Always   *Sometimes*   *Seldom*

5. I answer my phone promptly—when possible before or during the second ring.

   Always   *Sometimes*   *Seldom*

6. I am courteous to all callers and thank them for calling before ending the conversation.

   Always   *Sometimes*   *Seldom*

7. I **listen sympathetically** to callers and offer to be helpful.

   Always   *Sometimes*   *Seldom*

8. In order to establish a personal relationship, I use the caller's name often.

   Always   *Sometimes*   *Seldom*

9. If I must leave the line for more than a minute, I offer to return the call.

   Always   *Sometimes*   *Seldom*

10. I return all calls promptly unless there is a good reason not to do so.

    Always   *Sometimes*   *Seldom*

11. I treat all types of messages as important calls.

    Always   *Sometimes*   *Seldom*

12. When I take phone messages for others, I write down all the facts and put a date and time of day on the note before delivering it.

    Always   *Sometimes*   *Seldom*

13. I treat phone calls for others in the same courteous manner I would a call for myself.

    Always   *Sometimes*   *Seldom*

14. Before leaving my phone, I tell others where I can be reached and when I will return.

> *Always*   *Sometimes*   *Seldom*

15. I keep my calls brief and try to initiate the end of a conversation before the other party does it.

> *Always*   *Sometimes*   *Seldom*

16. I am able to cut off a long-winded speaker gracefully, without being offensive.

> *Always*   *Sometimes*   *Seldom*

17. I speak directly into the telephone.

> *Always*   *Sometimes*   *Seldom*

18. I am "other oriented" when speaking on the phone; that is, I try to be **empathetic** and understand the other party's point of view.

> *Always*   *Sometimes*   *Seldom*

19. I am aware of the impact that nonverbal behavior has on the tone of a call, and try to assume an appropriate physical and psychological posture.

> *Always*   *Sometimes*   *Seldom*

20. I speak at a slightly slower pace than usual when I am talking on the phone.

> *Always*   *Sometimes*   *Seldom*

21. I consciously try to use positive words and phrases on the telephone and avoid negative ones.

> *Always*   *Sometimes*   *Seldom*

22. I am a good listener when on the phone, using all the principles of active listening.

> *Always*   *Sometimes*   *Seldom*

23. I try not to interrupt other parties when they are speaking to me by phone.

> *Always*   *Sometimes*   *Seldom*

24. During an important call, I take notes to help support my memory of what was said.

> *Always*   *Sometimes*   *Seldom*

25. I am confident about speaking on the phone and approach telephone conversations with a positive mental attitude.

> *Always*   *Sometimes*   *Seldom*

Tabulating and Interpreting Your Test Score

Give yourself 4 points for every "Always" answer; 2 points for every "Sometimes"; no points for "Seldom". Add up your total.

Range	
100 (top score) to 92	You have earned an A. Congratulations! Use this book to sharpen your skills which are already quite good.
91 to 72	You are in the B–C range, which shows potential, but also indicates you have much to learn.
71 and below	HELP! You need to work hard mastering the content of this book in order to make yourself a potential valuable employee.

◤ ASSIGNMENTS FOR CHAPTER 1

1. Discuss what is meant by the following terms:
   a. information economy
   b. collapsing the information float

2. Discuss reasons why telephones are used more extensively in business today than in the past.

3. Look up *public relations* in a dictionary or encyclopedia. Discuss the meanings you find. Present specific ways that effective telephone use can help an employer's public relations image. How could it be harmed?

4. Explain how telephone communication differs from written communication. When is each appropriate or not appropriate?

5. Discuss the personality traits that might contribute to effective telephone skills. Name some that would not.

6. Write a short definition of these key words and phrases from chapter 1.
   Goodwill
   Personality
   Behavior listening
   Empathetic
   Sympathetic listening

> ## REVIEW QUIZ FOR CHAPTER 1

Indicate whether the following statements are true or false by circling your answer.

1. Sophisticated information technology has not changed the communications process.

   True   *False*

2. Much modern business relies on the exchange of instantaneous information.

   True   *False*

3. Written correspondence is no longer essential to business.

   True   *False*

4. By the year 2000, over one billion telephones will be connected to each other around the globe.

   True   *False*

5. According to George Walther, American business people spend as much time phoning as they do reading or doing paperwork.

   True   *False*

6. According to Nancy Friedman, every employee of an organization from janitor to president should be a skilled telephone user.

   True   *False*

7. Even as adults, we can change overt behaviors and acquire new skills.

   True   *False*

8. A recent survey indicates that corporate leaders consider telephone skills to be the most desired skills for employees to have.

   True   *False*

9. Most business telephone conversations are informal transactions.

   True   *False*

10. Most people consciously work at developing professional telephone skills.

    True   *False*

Four Principles of Telephone Communication

Learning Objectives

At the completion of this chapter, you will be able to

- Explain why the words we say and the way we say them are more important in telephone conversations than in face-to-face transactions.

- Define a Positive Mental Attitude (PMA).

- List ten ways that PMA can be used in telephone communication.

- Identify the similarities and differences between active listening tactics in telephone conversations and in face-to-face transactions.

- Recognize the interpersonal communications skills that should be used during telephone communication.

So far, we have concentrated on two important points:

1. The emphasis placed on telephone skills in today's business world.
2. The need to evaluate your own telephone personality to determine what skills you perform well and what skills you have to improve.

Now we will consider the four general principles of telephone communication. Once these four principles are clearly understood, you will be ready to begin learning and practicing the specific techniques that will help you reach your objective of becoming a skilled telephone communicator.

2.1   PRINCIPLE ONE: Telephone transactions rely more heavily on what words we say and the way we say them than do face-to-face transactions.

At first glance, this principle seems to be a self-evident truth, one that hardly requires analysis. That is not the case. To fully understand this idea, we must first examine the relative impact of the verbal and vocal parts of communication in face-to-face transactions. Fortunately, Albert Mehrabian has done the research for us, testing to find out how much the nonverbal, vocal, and verbal parts contribute to the total impact (100 percent) that we have on other people. The results usually surprise those not familiar with them.

Mehrabian's Total Impact Theory	
Body and other nonverbal	55%
Vocal (tone, pace, etc.)	38%
Verbal (words)	7%
Total Impact	100%

In other words, Mehrabian contends that more than 50 percent of the impression we make on others comes from our nonverbal modes of communication such as facial expressions, eye contact, body posture and movement, dress, use of space, and gestures. During telephone transactions, all of these nonverbal channels are missing. (Teleconferencing and picture phones are not yet widely used.) Simple logic forces us to conclude that during telephone transactions, the words we choose and the way in which we speak them are more important than they are in face-to-face encounters. Or, to say it another way, the person to whom you are speaking has only your words and your manner of speaking to form an impression of you.

To more fully realize this important point, take a few minutes to do this exercise. Write a paragraph describing a person you have spoken to by telephone, but have never met. Be specific; include a physical description as well as a personality profile. It is not important who the person is or what he or she does, but it is critical that you have never met.

_____

_____

_____

_____

_____

_____

_____

_____

_____

If you were able to form a composite description in the above exercise, remember that all of it resulted from the vocal and verbal impressions that person made on you. Ask yourself: What was the basis for your description? Your personality profile? The answers have to be the words and voice you heard.

If we were to adapt the Mehrabian Total Impact Theory to telephone communication, it might look something like this:

Vocal (tone, pace, etc.)	60%
Verbal (words)	40%
Total Impact	100%

What follows logically from Principle One is that you must concentrate much more on these two modes of communication when speaking on the telephone. They are all you have to offer. Keep this in mind when, later in this text, you are asked to learn and practice your telephone delivery and to use appropriate words and phrases to maximize your telephone effectiveness.

2.2 PRINCIPLE TWO: Bring a Positive Mental Attitude (PMA) to each telephone transaction.

Some ideas make so much sense, ring so true, and prove so effective that they endure and remain constant in an otherwise rapidly changing world. Such is the case with Principle Two. In their 1960 book, *Success Through a Positive Mental Attitude,* Napoleon Hill and W. Clement Stone offered these thoughts:

> A Positive Mental Attitude is a must for all who wish to make life pay off in their own terms. Nothing great was ever achieved without a positive mental attitude.

While it is true that PMA applies to all facets of our lives, it is not just a philosophical platitude or an abstract idea. Rather, it is a way of approaching everything we do in life, particularly the communication we have with others. Our telephone communications will be all the more productive and successful to the extent that we approach each one of them with a positive mental attitude.

Your positive mental attitude will spread to others, who will be attracted by your enthusiasm.

Just what is PMA? The authors of *Success Through a Positive Mental Attitude* define it this way:

> A **Positive Mental Attitude** is the right mental attitude for each given set of circumstances. It is most often comprised of the plus characteristics symbolized by such words as faith, integrity, hope, optimism, courage, initiative, generosity, tolerance, tact, kindliness, and good common sense.

To paraphrase the above definition and adapt it to our focus on telephone skills, PMA means approaching each telephone communication with a hopeful and confident attitude that is communicated to the other party through the words we use and the way we say them. Furthermore it means a willingness to give of ourselves in a straightforward way which will be contagious and lead to a productive and mutually beneficial exchange. Remember that PMA will not only lead to the successful accomplishment of your objectives, but it will spread to others who will be attracted by your enthusiasm.

Here are ten specific things you can do to begin practicing PMA in your telephone communications:

1. Psych yourself up before an important call. Much like an athlete before a contest, put yourself in a frame of mind that lets you visualize accomplishing your goal. Try it. It works!
2. Cultivate the habit of saying something, a sincere compliment or just a common courtesy, that will make the other party feel better.
3. Express an interest in or concern for the party with whom you are talking.
4. Let your voice show that you enjoy life. Sound happy.
5. Don't be afraid to laugh. It's the telephone equivalent of a smile.
6. Use positive language, words that people like.
7. Avoid being critical of others and making disparaging remarks.
8. Never argue over trivial matters. Even if you win the argument, you have gained little.

9. If the conversation doesn't work out as you wish, treat it as a learning experience from which you can profit.
10. End your conversation on a friendly, hopeful note.

2.3 PRINCIPLE THREE: Listening skills are as important as speaking skills during telephone communication.

Much attention has been given to "active listening" in recent years by both educational institutions and businesses. The source of the interest was the result of research conducted by Lyman K. Steil with University of Minnesota students. Steil's research confirmed that most people are ineffective listeners who retain only 50 percent of what they hear immediately after listening to a message and whose retention slips to 25 percent forty-eight hours later. Such statistics woke up American businesses who worried about the effect of poor listening on productivity. In response, communications consultants and educators wrote books and designed training sessions to increase listening effectiveness. While all of these efforts have considerable merit, they were largely directed at face-to-face communications and rarely to telephone exchanges. Although many of the suggestions to improve listening apply to both kinds of communications, there are differences which require different strategies.

First, let's review the face-to-face listening strategies that are common to telephone listening.

1. Don't interrupt the person to whom you are speaking unless absolutely necessary. If two people are speaking at the same time, neither one is listening. Be patient. Your chance to speak will come. In the interim, work at active listening.
2. Expend energy—work hard at what you are doing. You need to *feel* the effort. Active listening requires concentration, which is easier if you maintain an alert, attentive posture just as you would if your communication were face-to-face.
3. Don't pass judgment on the message too quickly. Be open-minded and resist quick, negative reactions which will get in the way of your listening to the rest of the message.

These strategies are the same for effective listening whether it takes place in person or on the telephone. However, there are also some different tactics that have to be used for good telephone listening.

1. Provide sufficient oral **feedback** to substitute for the nonverbal feedback you would normally offer face-to-face. Instead of an attentive posture, an interested facial expression, and eye contact, you should restate ideas and make statements that indicate your attention and understanding. Examples of this type of feedback might be quite simple: "I understand your point of view and agree with it," or "I am clear as to what you are saying and particularly support your last point."
2. Ask clarifying questions to prevent problems of misinterpretation. Without nonverbal signals to reinforce meaning, it is much easier to be uncertain about the intent of what is being said. If there is any doubt in your mind as to what the speaker means, ask for a clarification. "Do

Listening skills are as important as speaking skills during telephone communication.

I understand correctly that you wish to have us ship you the same order that we did at this time last year?"

3. Take notes that highlight the major points that were made. Note taking is the most effective way to increase retention of what you hear. Think of note taking as an advantage of telephone communication, an opportunity that is often inappropriate during face-to-face communication. Note taking is also the primary way you can offset the difficulties of understanding caused by the lack of nonverbal signals.

2.4   PRINCIPLE FOUR: Use basic interpersonal communication skills during telephone communication.

We all know people who are skilled in face-to-face communication but whose personalities seems to change when they pick up the telephone. They lose their effectiveness and are somehow different, less comfortable. If you are such a person, you need to remind yourself that many of the behaviors that work well for you in face-to-face communication apply to telephone communication as well. Here are some suggestions to help you achieve effective telephone behaviors.

1. Understand the purpose of each phone call you make and plan accordingly. Know the points you wish to make and how you intend to make them. Here, a notepad will come in handy again. Jot down the subjects you plan to discuss and the likely order in which they will be discussed. Notes will serve as a reminder and help avoid making an embarrassing second call should your memory fail you.
2. Be **other-oriented,** not self-oriented. Here, empathy is the key word, the ability to understand another person's point of view. Suppress your natural instinct to think of yourself first and be genuinely interested in and concerned about the other person. Use *You* more often than *I*. The response you will receive will be warm and positive.
3. Communicate for the future as well as the present. Business relationships often shift and change in unpredictable ways. Today's subordinate may

be an administrator tomorrow. A poor prospect may turn out to be your best customer. With this in mind, conduct telephone exchanges expecting that they will be long-lasting relationships. This means observing basic courtesies and keeping emotional reactions to a minimum.

4. Make your nonverbal behavior consistent with what you are saying and how you are saying it. Despite the fact that you cannot be seen, sit forward in an open, alert posture, have paper and pen ready for note taking, and assume an amiable facial expression. This set of nonverbal behaviors will come through in your oral delivery and will be "heard" if not "seen" by the other party. The reverse of this is also true. A closed, overly relaxed posture or a gloomy facial expression will most certainly have a negative effect on your delivery.

5. Make sure that the time you spend on the telephone is used as efficiently and productively as possible. Here again, the casual habits of our youth may need to be changed and replaced with techniques that demonstrate your understanding that in the world of business, the cliche, "time is money," is, in fact, true.

6. Be certain the physical setting where you conduct most of your phone calls is conducive to effective communication. If it is not, change it. Your telephone workplace should be quiet and free from noisy distractions and interruptions. In short, it should be designed to enhance your ability to use the telephone with maximum effectiveness.

These last two points are such important points and so often neglected that they will be dealt with in greater detail in the next chapter. However, before moving ahead to consider the importance of time and place in telephoning, review the general principles of telephone communication once more:

Principle One: Telephone transactions rely more heavily on what words we say and the way we say them than do face-to-face transactions.

Principle Two: Bring a Positive Mental Attitude (PMA) to each telephone transaction.

Principle Three: Listening skills are as important as speaking skills during telephone communications.

Principle Four: Use basic interpersonal communication skills during telephone communications.

► ASSIGNMENTS FOR CHAPTER 2

1. Discuss the variety of ways that telephone communication differs from face-to-face communication.

2. Based on your present telephone behavior, how might someone else (who has never met you) picture you? Write a paragraph imagining what his or her physical description and personality profile of you would be like.

3. Discuss other areas of your life in which a Positive Mental Attitude (PMA) would be helpful. Are you presently a person who emphasizes the positive or negative aspects of life? Why?

4. Discuss some reasons why most people are not good listeners. How can you tell when someone is not listening to you during a phone conversation?

5. Write a brief description of what your nonverbal behavior should be like during a business telephone conversation. Explain why.

6. Write a short definition of these key words and phrases from chapter 2.
Other-oriented
Feedback
Interpersonal communication skills
Mehrabian's Total Impact Theory
Positive Mental Attitude (PMA)

REVIEW QUIZ FOR CHAPTER 2

Indicate whether the following statements are true or false by circling your answer.

1. According to Albert Mehrabian, nonverbal modes of communication have a greater impact than verbal modes in face-to-face encounters.

    True   *False*

2. During a phone conversation, what words you say and the way you say them account for the total impact you make.

    True   *False*

3. You should prepare yourself for important phone calls just as you would for an athletic event.

    True   *False*

4. Listening tests at the University of Minnesota confirm that most people retain only 75 percent of what they hear immediately after listening to a message.

    True   *False*

5. Retention is greater in telephone listening than in face-to-face encounters.

    True   *False*

6. Being open-minded is one of the keys to effective listening.

    True   *False*

7. Taking notes is one of the best ways to help retention during phone conversations.

    True   *False*

8. Since there is no visual contact during telephone conversations, the posture we assume is not relevant in any way.

    True   *False*

9. Some people are more comfortable in face-to-face encounters than when talking on the telephone.

    True   *False*

10. Oral feedback may substitute for nonverbal feedback during telephone conversations.

    True   *False*

Time, Place, and Telephoning

Learning Objectives

At the completion of the chapter, you will be able to

■ Explain how time-management principles can be applied to the use of the office telephone.

■ Identify four telephone behaviors that are common time-wasters.

■ Identify four telephone behaviors that are effective time-savers.

■ Describe three characteristics of a suitable telephone workplace and suggest three ways of creating such an environment in an open office.

■ List the items that are needed in order for a telephone workplace to be functionally equipped.

3.1   INTRODUCTION

At the end of the previous chapter, you were urged to apply basic inter-personal communications skills to your telephone usage (Principle Four). The last two suggestions for achieving these skills need to be repeated here:

5. Make sure that the time you spend on the telephone is used as efficiently and productively as possible.
6. Be certain the physical setting where you conduct most of your phone calls is conducive to effective communication. If it is not, change it.

You can learn all the other phone skills treated in this book and still not be successful as a business telephone user if you do not master these two points. Put in other words, you must learn how to *manage* the time that you spend on the telephone, not just use it. Furthermore, you should understand why the most successful telephone exchanges take place in a workplace which contributes to that success.

3.2   MANAGING YOUR TELEPHONE TIME

Time-management has generated considerable interest among corporate leaders in recent years. The reason for this is clear. American workers need to increase their efficiency and productivity if their companies are to compete in a global economy. The effective use of time can be a major step toward achieving these goals. In addition, time-management techniques also reduce the stress and anxiety caused by wasting time.

Typically, **time-management principles** can be broken down to two ideas: (1) developing a personal work plan, and (2) sticking to that plan. Work plans can be made for a day, a week, a month, or more. Planning often involves making lists of tasks that can be crossed off when completed or carried over to the next list if not yet done. There is no secret to time-management principles; they are just commonsense ways to get the most productivity out of the time that you are at work.

American business people make 500,000,000 telephone calls per day according to communications analysts. The potential for wasted time is enormous; therefore, the need for efficient use of telephone time is obvious. All that is needed is the application of time-management skills to telephone use.

Managing your telephone time simply means applying time-management principles to your use of the office telephone. In other words, develop a personal work plan that includes a specific plan for telephone use and stick to the plan. Here are some specific ways to make use of the general ideas discussed above.

1. *Organize most of your phone calls so that they can be made all at the same time.*
   If you are a secretary, this may mean encouraging your supervisor to plan phone calls and assisting with the organization process. Mark McCormack, the well-known sports management agent, supports this approach in his book, *What They Don't Teach You at Harvard Business School:*

DAILY WORK PLAN

8:00	*Staff Meeting in Conference Room.*		
9:00	*Read and answer mail.*		
10:00	*Return Calls:*	*F. Jacobs*	*call: Ryan Paper*
		R. Stern	*Jim Gilbert*
		W. Williams	*Ann Strong*
11:00	*Interview—Joan Barr*		
12:00	*Lunch—Clients from Flint Advertising*		

I can pretty well estimate how long it will take me to make all my phone calls on a particular day. If I have promised to return a call at a specific time, I will make that call very close to when I said I would. For all remaining calls, I will allocate a time period, usually thirty to ninety minutes, and set that time aside.

As you can see, McCormack develops a personal time plan for handling most of the phone calls he has to make. What is important here, even if it is only implied, is that such a time plan frees the rest of the day to handle other business matters.

2. *Plan your phone calls for times that maximize your chances of reaching the other party.*

Do you know that approximately 75 percent of business calls are not completed on the first attempt? If not, you do now, and you can easily figure out that continuous callbacks are time-consuming. Is there a way to increase your chances of reaching the other party? Are some times better to make calls than others? The answer is YES to both questions. Research shows that you can increase your chances of completing your phone calls by calling in the mornings from Tuesday to Friday. The worst time to make connections is on Monday morning or near the end of a work day. These times should be avoided unless the call is absolutely necessary.

Having made these general statements about the best and worst times to make calls, we need to acknowledge exceptions to the rules. In fact, a person's availability often is directly linked to his or her occupation. For example, contractors usually are at job sites early in the morning, lawyers appear in courtrooms in the mornings, and college faculty teach at odd hours throughout the day. What you need to do is to ask a simple question, "What is a good time to call?" Put the answer in a tickler system and refer to it for future calls.

3. *Plan time off for short breaks from constant telephoning.*

This is an important point for switchboard operators, customer service representatives, and other employees who spend most of their time interacting with the public. Their planning must include breaks—time off from constant telephone communication. Without planned breaks to look forward to, burnout occurs, employees become impatient with angry callers, and the quality of communication suffers.

This is especially true if you have to handle complaints on a regular basis. Manage stress by taking minibreaks in addition to your scheduled breaks. Get up from your desk, take a short walk, visit with a fellow employee, anything that will break the pattern of complaints you have to handle. It may only take a few seconds, but it will help you cope with **job stress**—anxiety—more successfully.

In addition to these suggestions, time management also means avoiding telephone habits that waste time.

3.3 TIME-WASTERS

One of the wasteful habits employers most discourage is the use of the office telephone for personal calls. Most companies will permit calls for emergencies or other important reasons if those calls are kept brief. However, the general rule against personal calls exists for two very good reasons. If you are socializing on the phone, you are not doing other work; and, at the same time, business callers cannot reach your number. Nothing irritates a supervisor more than if he/she is out of the office and unable to reach a secretary because the phone is being used for personal reasons. When that occurs, it is quite common for the supervisor to begin calling the office just to see if the phone is free.

Small talk is another common squanderer of time. Yes, social pleasantries have a place in business communication, but they should occur after business is done and, even then, only when both parties have the time. George Walther agrees with this suggestion:

> Consider beginning important business calls with a quick overview of the main subjects you plan to cover. Reach agreement with the other person item by item. With your objectives achieved and business out of the way, you can enjoy small talk. Business first; then the informal exchanges that cement our long-term business relationships.

It is important that a distinction be made here. By small talk, we do not mean the basic courtesies that are appropriate at the beginning of a call, such as asking how someone has been or inquiring about the timing of the call. Such courtesies are expected. "Small talk" here refers to longer, nonbusiness chats about family, golf scores, vacations, and the like.

Experts agree that the most common telephone time-waster is lack of proper call **preparation**:

> Inadequate preparation for a telephone call can cause more than mere delay; it means the call must be placed again. Misconnections and incomplete calls can be costly and are frustrating for both you and the people you may interrupt. Careful preparation enables you to use your telephone efficiently and do your job effectively.

Consider this. It is unlikely that you would make a business call in person without first planning your objective and the items you wished to discuss. It follows, then, that in an age when more and more business is being

> **CALL TO** *Mary Hayes*
>
> **Purpose:** *To track December shipment.*
>
> **1.** *Inquire about timing of call.*
> **2.** *Ask about December order.*
> **3.** *When was it shipped?*
> **4.** *At what discount? (15% last year)*
> **5.** *When will new styles be available?*

transacted by phone, similar preparation is required. Try this. For all important phone calls, write down your objective or purpose. What is it you wish to accomplish by this call? Below the statement of purpose, jot down the points you wish to cover in the logical order you would like to discuss them. Include any relevant facts or statistics you wish to use. That is preparation. See if it works.

Other time-wasters include putting callers on hold for excessive lengths of time or transferring calls haphazardly because you do not know how to handle the caller's problem. The conscientious employee will become knowledgeable enough about the company's business so that he or she may handle many situations personally or transfer the call to the party from whom satisfaction may be obtained. This also includes becoming totally familiar with the telephone equipment being used.

3.4   TIME-SAVERS

In addition to the suggestions made above, here are some additional ways to conserve telephone time.

1. *When you call someone, inquire about the timing of your call to see if you have interrupted something important.*
   You have no way of knowing what the other person is doing. It may be a bad time to call, and this may in fact stop you from achieving your objective unless you ask, "Is this a good time for you to talk?" Besides, this approach shows you care about the other person.

2. *Place your own outgoing phone calls.*
   Telephone companies recommend that everyone should place his or her own phone calls. Having secretaries or office assistants place calls for supervisors is out-of-date and inefficient, a real time-waster.

3. *Once your business is done, try to bring the call to an end before the other party does it.*
   Once again, courtesy comes first. "I have enjoyed talking with you, Mrs. Walker, but I know you are busy also. I will send you the information you requested immediately."

4. *When receiving calls, answer promptly, preferably between the first and second ring.*

This not only saves time but creates the positive impression of a company and employee alert and eager to do business. The opposite of this is also true, of course. If a business phone is left unanswered after four or five rings, the caller may form negative ideas of an understaffed company whose people are indifferent to customers or client needs. Although it may be standard practice for adolescents at home to deliberately let the phone ring for fear of ruining their casual image, it is just the opposite in business. Pick up that phone as soon as you can and get on with a productive exchange.

5. *Prepare thoroughly before each call.*

Thorough preparation protects against memory lapses and the need for further calls, which are both expensive and embarrassing.

Note: The screening of incoming calls by switchboard operators and secretaries—or even answering machines and voice-mail systems—is a commonly accepted practice today. Screening allows those who receive many calls to regulate the flow of those calls most efficiently. In some cases, a person screening calls may be able to redirect the call to another party for proper handling, or a secretary may be able to satisfy the callers request personally. In other situations, the purpose of the screen may be just to let the supervisor know in advance who is calling and for what purpose. You will be shown how to use various screening methods and how to avoid telephone tag in Chapter 6.

3.5 CONSTRUCTING A SUITABLE TELEPHONE WORKPLACE

Now that the relationship of time and telephone skills is clear to you, point 6 of Principle Four in chapter 2 needs to be explored. To refresh your memory:

6. Be certain the physical setting where you conduct most of your phone calls is conducive to effective communication. If it is not, change it.

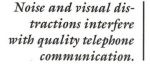
Noise and visual distractions interfere with quality telephone communication.

Today companies go to considerable effort and expense in selecting the right phone systems for their business. Suppliers of phone systems offer a wide variety of equipment that ranges from basic to state-of-the-art in complexity and sophistication. However, it is often unaccountably ironic that once having chosen a quality system, companies allow the telephones themselves to be placed in the worst possible settings for communication.

A case in point occurred at a small midwestern college where a friend of mine teaches. Faculty were provided phones in their offices, but those phones were limited to local calls only. To make professional calls outside of the local area, a faculty phone was provided in the busy academic affairs office. The phone was placed in a part of the office that was heavily trafficked, and a radio blasted out music from a shelf above the phone. Faculty complained of distractions, inability to hear, and the lack of privacy. Finally, when frustrations and negative feelings peaked, a phone was provided in a faculty resource room that was both quiet and private.

This example emphasizes three major characteristics that are necessary if quality communication is going to occur. A **telephone workplace** must be quiet, free from most distractions, and afford some degree of privacy. Obviously, it is easier to accomplish these objectives if you have a private office. However, many receptionists, secretaries, and other service people work in open, outer offices where creating a suitable telephone environment is more of a challenge. In these situations, try these suggestions.

A telephone workplace should be quiet, free from distractions, and functionally equipped to help get the job done.

1. Arrange your furniture so that traffic immediately around your telephone workplace is kept to a minimum.
2. Position the phone so that **visual distractions** from around the office are as few as possible.
3. Get rid of radios and the like that impede your ability to hear. Also, politely let the people around you know that you need quiet in order to carry on phone conversations.

Besides having suitable surroundings, a telephone workplace must also be functionally equipped to help get the job done. At the minimum, this means having pencils, pens, and notepads to be used exclusively for preparatory notes (discussed earlier in this chapter.) Printed message slips which allow you to take and leave messages for others should be handy. Also, list of frequently called numbers along with company and public directories should be within reach. The latter should include alphabetical directories, classified directories, and special directories such as the *AT&T 800 Toll-Free Directory,* which can be both useful and economical.

Customer service representatives and others, who work on the telephone all day may require chairs that provide proper support for their backs. To counter boredom, some companies may create some visual stimuli by bringing in plants or hanging pictures and paintings. Some companies even ask their telephone representatives to set up mirrors as a way of checking nonverbal behavior, which invariably influences communication. Other service people request telephone cords of extra length so they can explore files for information without putting the caller on hold. The possibilities are endless, but the message is simple. Create a workplace that is helpful to productivity.

Of course, much more in the way of equipment and services can be had today. These will vary with employment situations, and training will customarily be provided to employees. It is not our purpose to discuss all available options here, but many offices will employ speaker phones, answering machines, teleconferencing capabilities, and other more advanced equipment.

ASSIGNMENTS FOR CHAPTER 3

1. Discuss two ways that time-management principles could be applied to telephone communication in a typical work week.

2. Cite four common ways that employees waste time by their telephone behavior.

3. Discuss ways to prepare for important phone calls. What is the purpose of call preparation? What might preparation prevent?

4. List the items necessary to equip a telephone workplace.

5. Describe the ideal telephone workplace.

6. Write a short definition of the following key words and phrases from chapter 3.
   Time management principles
   Job stress
   Call preparation

Telephone workplace

Visual distractions

▶ R E V I E W   Q U I Z   F O R   C H A P T E R   3

Indicate whether the following statements are true or false by circling your answer.

1. American workers need to improve efficiency and productivity so that our companies will be able to compete in a global economy.

       True   *False*

2. Stress and anxiety can sometimes be caused by poor use of time.

       True   *False*

3. It is a fact that 90 percent of business calls are not completed on the first attempt.

       True   *False*

4. One of the best times to make business phone calls is on Monday mornings.

       True   *False*

5. Planned breaks are necessary for switchboard operators in order to avoid burnout.

       True   *False*

6. Small talk should be saved for the end of business phone conversations.

       True   *False*

7. Lack of proper preparation before placing a call is the number-one telephone time-waster.

       True   *False*

8. Phones should be answered between the second and third ring.

       True   *False*

9. Notepads are vital to effective telephone use.

       True   *False*

10. Quality telephone communication requires a suitable environment in which to occur.

       True   *False*

4

Using New Technology

Learning Objectives

At the completion of this chapter, you will be able to

- List the benefits and concerns associated with mobile car phones.

- Explain how voice mail can be an effective supplement to personal telephone communication.

- Describe the appropriate use for fax machines in business communications.

- Define electronic mail and explain how computer users communicate with this new medium.

- Recognize the advantages of conference calls.

In chapter 1, you read about the "collapsing of the information float," the way that more sophisticated information technology is creating a faster flow of information in the information channel. New technology not only speeds up the flow of information, but often changes the very nature and type of communication that takes place. Interactive television is a clear example of this kind of revolutionary change.

Similar transformations have been occurring in the workplace, dramatically altering patterns of business communication. Some of the more significant technological developments are mobile calls, voice mail, fax machines, electronic mail (E-mail), and conference calls. Employees who wish to keep current must familiarize themselves with each of the new communication tools so that they may use each appropriately and to best advantage.

4.1 MOBILE CALLS

Cellular telephone technology has developed rapidly in recent years. This remarkable combination of telephone and radio technology has dramatically changed the way that business people use their travel and leisure time. Telephones are now commonly available in the coach and first class sections on commercial aircraft. Boaters and golfers are no longer cut off from business communication, and soon the man on the street will be dialing clients from portable, hand-held telephones. While these breakthroughs are important, the most significant change has been the widespread use of the mobile car phone. Today, companies and individuals must consider the role that mobile car phones can play in increasing productivity.

Advantages of Mobile Car Telephones

The arguments for mobile car phones are very direct and very convincing. Proponents of car phones quote business management experts who claim that the secret to success is improving personal productivity. Productivity is directly connected to how we utilize our time, and car phones allow us to transform previously unproductive time to productive time.

Some studies estimate that people who drive to work can gain as much as two hours each working day, a 25% increase in potentially productive time. This benefit is not only for professional people as there are advantages for sales, delivery, or service people as well. Time wasted driving and parking simply to find pay phones can be converted to more profitable activities. The cliche that "time is money" holds true and becomes a strong argument for mobile car phones.

Cost and Safety

Once the benefits of mobile car phones are acknowledged, consideration and attention need to be given to the questions of cost and safety. As business investments, car phones are not for everyone. There must be clear evidence that having a mobile phone will permit an individual to be sufficiently more productive in order to justify the cost of the equipment. This will vary by company and individual, but ultimately it requires an individual to estimate what his/her time is worth. Once that is determined, a direct comparison can be made with the cost of the car phone to see if the expense is justified.

Mobile car phones can play a role in increasing productivity.

Finally, business people planning to use mobile car phones must take precautions to ensure that the telephone transaction doesn't jeopardize the primary activity of driving safely. Common sense is the best guide, but it also helps to drive more slowly when making calls, to keep calls brief, and to dial only when stopped for lights or when traffic is minimal. Keep in mind that the four principles of telephone communication discussed in chapter 2 also apply to mobile telephone communication.

4.2   VOICE MAIL

Technology is changing telephone communication inside offices as well as outside. Major telephone companies now offer many different services that businesses can select for their employees. One of the most useful services is voice mail, a telephone answering service that stores messages and uses a signal to alert employees that a message is waiting in the voice mailbox. Employees are able to erase the message from the voice mail's computer system after hearing the message, or they can retain it for future reference.

Properly used, voice mail can be a communications asset. Ideally, voice mail activates when all phone systems are busy or no one is in the office to answer calls personally. Callers can still leave messages with important content or simply ask that their call be returned.

Problems occur when voice mail is overused or misused. Callers quickly become frustrated when their efforts to make a personal business contact are met only with recorded messages. Effective communicators realize this and try to minimize the use of voice mail, realizing it is intended to be a *supplement,* not a replacement for live personal communication.

4.3   FAX MACHINES

The fax machine is perhaps the clearest example of a technological tool that is in step with the times. During the early 1990s, fax machines appeared everywhere; it seemed no business was complete without one. Even individuals who could not afford their own machine could send and receive fax messages from their local business centers for a small fee. Fax machines extend the "collapse of the information float" even further (see chapter 1), and satisfy a public impatient to exchange business information.

Fax machines have this broad appeal because they allow users to transmit printed pictures of written copy or graphics immediately to a second party with a receiving fax machine. "Fax it to me" has become a standard part of today's business jargon.

As is the case with all the new technological communications supplements, fax machines must be used appropriately. When time can be saved by faxing important information or urgently needed written records, faxing is the method to choose. Too often however, fax machines are used for commonplace communications for which there is no pressing need. Such material is better sent through interoffice or regular mails. In all cases, the sender should choose the most suitable and cost-efficient medium of communication for the message being delivered. Fax machines are a major advancement, but they are not intended to replace more traditional forms of communication such as business letters or telephone calls.

Fax machines have extended the collapse of the information float.

4.4   ELECTRONIC MAIL

One of the fastest growing new forms of communication is electronic mail, or E-mail, a system in which senders type messages on computer screens. The messages are sent via data circuits run by major commercial networks such as CompuServe or America Online. Users of these services can now connect with one another through Internet, the computer linking service that allows users on one system to communicate with users on other systems. According to the Electronic Mail Association in Washington, DC, there are now 25 million users nationwide who now have access to E-mail through their computer modems at work or at home.

Both E-mail and fax machine communications are written messages and require different skills than oral telephone communication. However, they share some characteristics with oral communication. For example, privacy cannot always be guaranteed, a fact which must be considered. The major limitation of E-mail is that it can only be used by fellow computer users and then only when you have the correct computer addresses. Undoubtedly, these limitations will be overcome as the technology becomes more refined.

4.5   CONFERENCE CALLS

Some new technology offers businesses substantial savings and increased efficiency. Conference calling, which allows three or more persons at different locations (across the country—or across the world) to talk on the same telephone connection, is an example of this type of technology. Whether the conference call is arranged with the assistance of an operator or with specially installed equipment, it can be a major improvement in business communication when conducted properly.

To be successful, conference calls must be directed by one person, just as any successful meeting needs a leader or chairperson. He or she should state what is to be discussed during the call and be sure that all parties have their chance to talk. To be productive, all participants should have advance notice of the conference call in order that they can properly prepare and gather information. Conference calls can save considerable time and expense, allowing group decisions to be made without requiring all parties to come together from different locales.

ASSIGNMENTS FOR CHAPTER 4

1. Present the major argument supporting the use of mobile car phones for business.

2. Explain the most appropriate uses of voice mail.

3. Explain what is meant by the statement that fax machines extend "the collapse of the information float."

4. What key function does Internet perform?

5. Discuss the similarities that conference calls have with ordinary business meetings.

6. Write a short definition of these key words and phrases from chapter 4.

mobile calls   voice mail

fax machines   electronic mail

conference calls

▶ REVIEW QUIZ FOR CHAPTER 4

Indicate whether the following statements are true or false by circling your answer.

1. Cellular telephone technology is a combination of telephone and radio technology.

       True   *False*

2. Personal productivity is directly connected to how we utilize our time.

       True   *False*

3. Car phones should be standard equipment for all business people.

       True   *False*

4. Effective communicators try to minimize the use of voice mail.

       True   *False*

5. Fax machines are intended to replace the personal business telephone call.

       True   *False*

6. Fax machines offer immediate transmission of printed pictures of written copy or graphics.

       True   *False*

7. Internet links major commercial computer networks with one another.

       True   *False*

8. One limitation of E-mail is that it is only available to computer users.

       True   *False*

9. Conference calls allow two persons to talk on the same telephone connection.

       True   *False*

10. Conference calls should be arranged in advance with all participants.

       True   *False*

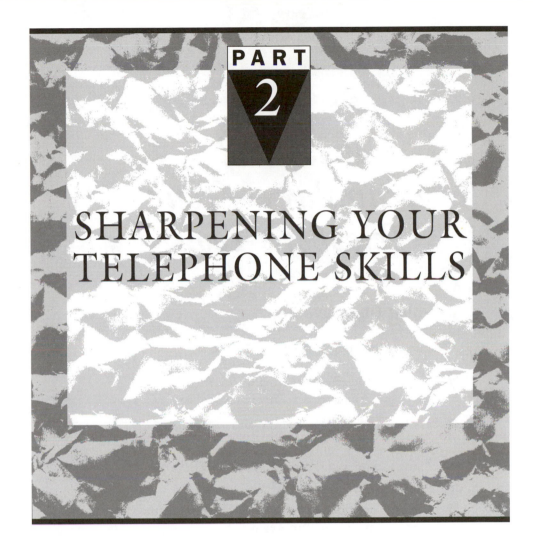

PART
2

SHARPENING YOUR TELEPHONE SKILLS

CHAPTER
5

Voice and Vocabulary—Your Telephone Tools

Learning Objectives

At the completion of this chapter, you will be able to

■ Speak on the telephone in a warm, friendly voice that communicates a positive personality.

■ Use the appropriate volume and pace when speaking on the telephone.

■ Choose words and phrases that contribute to productive telephone exchanges.

■ Begin telephone conversations with phrases that make a positive first impression.

■ Conclude telephone conversations tactfully.

Part 1 of this text (chapters 1–4) presented a theoretical basis for helping you to understand telephone communication more clearly. Specifically, you learned the significant role of the telephone in today's business world, the personality traits that are helpful in telephone use, the basic principles of telephone communication, and the importance of managing your telephone time and the place in which you conduct your telephone transactions.

Now, it is time for you to take on a more active role as you *learn and practice* those skills that will make you a successful telephone communicator. To begin, you need to return to Principle One of telephone communication that you learned in chapter 2.

> Principle One—Telephone transactions rely more heavily on what words we say and the way we say them than do face-to-face transactions.

Reread the discussion of that principle in chapter 2 to prepare you to begin mastering voice and vocabulary, two essential telephone tools.

Not only must you understand the ideas discussed in Part 2, but you must also do the exercises designed to strengthen specific skills.

5.1 VOICE AND PERSONALITY

While I was writing this book, I asked friends and acquaintances to tell me of any business telephone experiences they had had that might be instructive to readers. One woman shared this anecdote.

Several summers ago, my friend made a decision to make a modest investment in mutual funds of a particular type. She read financial journals and narrowed her choice to four specific funds. She then called the 800 phone numbers of the funds to request a prospectus and an application from each. All four customer service representatives answered their phones in a similar way and requested essentially the same information from her. The first three customer representatives were enthusiastic, warm, and friendly. The last was disinterested, cold, and impersonal. My friend made a decision on the spot not to invest her money in the last fund, and when the prospectus arrived, she glanced at it only briefly before discarding it. Ultimately, she decided to split her investment between two of the other three funds.

You may argue that investment decisions shouldn't be based on the personality of a customer service representative, and you may be right. However, hers was a very human reaction, and I suspect many other people make business decisions for the same reasons. Remember the key points in this example. Each customer representative *said very much the same words, but the way they said what they said was different*. In other words, voices revealed personalities that she, the customer, either liked or disliked.

The idea that voice and personality are inseparable during telephone communication needs to be reinforced. Writing in a *Wall Street Journal* article, "Your Telephone Voice May Be Working Against You," Ralph Proodian makes a strong case:

> Millions are spent each year on business dinners, shows, and drinks to gain mutual trust, win contracts, and close deals. Yet telephone communication, the power tool of our service economy, is abused by voices that squawk, groan,

chirp, squeak, and mutter. All those books and seminars on how to use body language are useless when talking blind through a phone line. And what you put in comes out at the other end even worse.

Proodian, a New York-based speech consultant and assistant professor of speech at Brooklyn College, goes on to make the point that the standard telephone may transmit tones of voice that may misrepresent you and convey messages to the listener that are unintended.

Before we offer suggestions about how to have your voice communicate a positive personality, we need to examine what personality traits you want your voice to transmit. There is general agreement that the ideal telephone voice should do the following:

1. Be warm, friendly and, at the same time, businesslike. Breathy Madonna imitations have no place in business, nor do macho Clint Eastwood or Rambo sound-alikes.
2. Be confident—use a tone of voice that expresses a "can do" attitude.
3. Be clear and **enunciate** words well to avoid possible misunderstandings.
4. Be courteous, helpful, and sincere.
5. Be interested and enthusiastic, and let your voice say you enjoy doing your job well.

Voice and personality are inseparable during telephone communication.

To acquire such a telephone voice, you must first examine the manner in which you presently speak on the phone. Understand that your present voice is partly a result of biology and partly of environment. That is to say, your own physical makeup, including your vocal cords and larynx, influences the way you sound. Besides biology, environmental factors play a large role. If you grew up in Birmingham, Alabama, your voice will have a different pace and tone than someone from the Bronx in New York. The way your parents spoke, as well as any speech training you may have had, will also play a role. Finally, your voice will change depending on how well you are feeling or how tired you are.

Once you have taken stock of your present voice, you can make some attitude adjustments, employ specific nonverbal behaviors, and then practice, practice, practice the recommended techniques.

Attitude change comes first. The switchboard operator, secretary, customer service representative, or administrative assistant whose voice conveys winning characteristics is usually a person who understands the importance of his or her role. These people work hard at making positive **first impressions,** realizing that business may be gained or lost based on their performance. They adopt a Positive Mental Attitude (chapter 3), psych themselves up before answering or placing calls, and then let their voices reflect the way they feel. Not surprisingly, these same people often reap benefits in their personal lives as others respond to their enthusiasm.

Earlier, the point was made that despite the fact that you are not engaged in face-to-face encounters when using the telephone, your nonverbal behavior comes through in your oral delivery and will be "heard," if not seen, by the other party. An alert, open posture—one where you sit forward, uncross your arms and legs, and are prepared to take notes—will almost certainly trigger a positive tone of voice. Finally, the effectiveness of your telephone voice (and personality) is also influenced by the volume of your speech and the rate at which you speak.

5.2 VOLUME AND PACE

The volume at which you speak can help or hurt the success of your communication. If you speak too loudly, you are likely to irritate the listener or come across as inconsiderate or boorish. If your voice is too soft, you project an insecure, nonassertive image of yourself. Both extremes risk the possibility of contributing to misunderstandings. If you are uncertain about your volume, check it out. Ask a friend "Am I speaking too loud?" or "Is my voice too low?"

Obviously, the best volume is a comfortable midpoint between the two extremes that approximates your natural speaking voice. The best way to achieve this is to hold the mouthpiece about two inches from your mouth. Today's telephones carry your voice at the speed of light, and you do not have to increase your volume just because you are speaking to someone in another part of the country—or even another country. If, however, you have an unusually soft voice, you may have to move the mouthpiece closer to compensate. One word of caution here; if you are too close to the receiver your words will be blurred and unclear.

Just as the right volume is critical to the voice, so too is **pace**—the rate at which you speak while on the phone. Once again, you wish to avoid speaking too rapidly or too slowly. Speaking quickly may create the impression that you know what you are talking about, but it also may put the listener on the defensive and, in certain circumstances, provoke distrust or suspicion. The expression "fast talker" suggests someone who is less than trustworthy, someone who may try to get the better of you. On the other hand, speaking too slowly creates another problem. Since the average person is able to comprehend spoken words at a rate of 500 words per minute, the listener may be left with a great deal of time in which attention may wander. If your rate of speech is less than the average of 125–250 words per minute, you risk losing the listener, especially since the nonverbal signals are not there to hold attention.

Given these two negative possibilities, the solution to the problem is not an easy one. It is too simplistic to say, speak at your natural rate, or keep your pace at a medium rate of speed. Most communication specialists suggest speaking at a slightly slower rate of speed when on the telephone. Their reasoning is that a slower rate ensures clarity and the listener's attention can be kept by being precise and brief. This makes good sense, but so too do George Walther's statements about pace. Walther suggests adapting your communication patterns, including volume and speaking rate, to the other party's patterns. If the other person speaks rapidly, you should mirror the pace and do so yourself. Walther argues that such a strategy establishes **rapport** between communicators. It may also be a matter of adapting to the circumstances of the call. In the real world of business, rate of speaking is often related to the sense of urgency of the business being transacted. Clearly a rate of speaking out of sync with the business situation is unacceptable. Putting these last two ideas together leads us to a sound conclusion as to what rate of speech should be used for telephone communication. In general, speak slightly slower than usual, but be prepared to adapt your rate to the other person or to the business situation itself.

Taping your telephone voice is a good way to improve your performance.

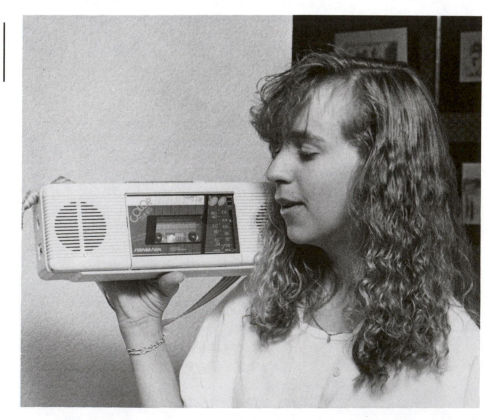

5.3 PRACTICING AND EVALUATING YOUR TELEPHONE VOICE

Developing a pleasing and professional telephone voice requires the same steps that were necessary to acquire any other skill you now possess. You must first be taught how to do something, then be given the opportunity to practice the skill; and you need to receive constructive criticism, some feedback as to how you are doing. So far in this chapter, you have learned the relationship between your voice and your telephone personality as well as the effect of volume and pace on your delivery.

Now you must take the next step. In this section, you are given short scripts to read aloud. The scripts simulate standard business conversations that occur frequently. Your instructor may conduct these exercises in class where you may benefit from the constructive criticism of your classmates. In addition you should practice at home with a tape recorder. Hearing your own voice is always fun and is sometimes an eye-opening experience. One publication, the "Telephone Selling Report," makes this suggestion: "Tape your voice at various times of the day when talking on the telephone. Then determine when your sound is at its best and its worst. Try to improve on the times when your voice doesn't seem as effective."

To assist you in the evaluation process, critique sheets are provided at the end of the exercise to remind you of the major points to check. Whether you are evaluating a classmate or yourself, try to be as honest as possible. Take the time to write down comments that will help you improve. The dialogue of the script allows you to concentrate on *how* you are speaking and not what you are saying. It might be helpful as you begin these exercises to remind yourself of your purpose. An old Bell System training manual said it best: "SOUND AS GOOD AS YOU REALLY ARE."

PRACTICE

EXERCISES

Simulated Telephone Conversations

Simulation 1   *You are an administrative assistant to Mr. Arthur Brown, the vice president of marketing for Smith Plastics Company. The following conversation takes place. For realism, use your own name where there are blanks.*

You: (*The telephone rings once*) "Good afternoon. Arthur Brown's office— [*name*] speaking: How may I help you?"

Caller: "Yes, may I speak with Mr. Brown, please?"

You: "May I tell Mr. Brown who's calling?"

Caller: "Certainly. This is Jane Givens of Acme Supply."

You: "Just one moment, I'll see if Mr. Brown is available."

Pause while caller is put on hold.

Caller: (*To Mr. Brown*) "You have a call from Jane Givens of Acme Supply."

Call is connected.

Simulation 2   *You are the receptionist-operator at the Kealy Tool Company. All incoming calls to the company come through your switchboard. The following conversation takes place.*

You: "Good morning—Kealy Tool Company."

Caller: "May I talk to your sales representative, George Dausey?"

You: "I'm sorry, Mr. Dausey is not in the office just now. May I help you?"

Caller: "No. I need to talk to Mr. Dausey concerning a problem with our last shipment of tools."

You: "If you give me your name and phone number, I will have Mr. Dausey return your call as soon as possible."

Caller: "This is Bill Richards of Richards Building, and my telephone number is (555) 295-5666."

You: "Thank you Mr. Richards. Your number is (555) 295-5666. I will give the message to Mr. Dausey. Thank you for calling."

Simulation 3   *You are a secretary in the Travel-Tourism Department at Central Community College. The following conversation takes place.*

You: *(The telephone rings once)* "Good morning.—Travel/Tourism Department—This is [*name*] speaking, may I help you?"

Caller: "Yes, I need some information about the kinds of programs that you offer. I'm considering returning to college."

You: "I'll be happy to be of assistance. Are you interested in being a day or evening student?"

Caller: "I work full-time, so I would be limited to your evening division."

You: "Fine. If you'll give me your name and address, I'll send you our Continuing Education catalogue immediately. It describes both the two- and four-year programs that are available in Travel/Tourism."

Caller: "My name is Ralph Penn, and I live at 10 Brook Street in Franklin, Massachusetts. My ZIP Code is 02943."

You: "Let me read this back to be certain I have it correct. You live at 10 Brook Street, Franklin, Massachusetts, ZIP Code 02943."

Caller: "Correct."

You: "I'll send the catalogue to you immediately, Mr. Penn. Thank you for your interest. Goodbye."

Simulation 4   *You are a customer service representative at Warner's Department Store. The following conversation takes place.*

You: "Good afternoon—Warner's Department Store—[*name*] speaking. How may I help you?"

Caller: (*Angry voice*) "Yes, I have a complaint I want handled immediately. Am I speaking to the right person?"

You: "Yes, I am here to try to help you. Could you give me your name and describe the problem?"

Caller: "My name is Burbank, Elsa Burbank. I'm calling about a toaster I bought to give as a wedding gift. I just received a call telling me the toaster never worked. I can't tell you how embarrassed I am."

You: "I understand, Ms. Burbank, and you can be sure I'll try to correct the problem. Would it be possible for you to bring the defective toaster to our Main Street store?"

Caller: "Well, that's not the most convenient thing for me to do, but I'll try."

You: "If you would be nice enough to do that, our customer service department will assist you. If the toaster is defective, they'll replace it or give you credit, whichever you prefer."

Caller: "I'll try to bring it in later this week."

You: "Thank you for being so understanding. We appreciate your business, and we will do whatever is necessary to correct the problem. Thank you for calling."

Simulation 5   *You are an administrative assistant at the Island Bank and Trust Company. The following conversation takes place.*

You: "Good afternoon—Island Bank and Trust—[*name*] speaking. How may I help you?"

Caller: "I would like some information on current mortgage rates. Can you help me?"

You: "Certainly. We have a variety of different mortgage instruments, which vary in rate depending on the type of mortgage you choose. May I suggest that you let me set up an appointment with one of our mortgage representatives to discuss the various options?"

Caller: "That sounds like a good idea. My name is Dr. Alvin Schneider, and I'm free Wednesday afternoons."

You: "Thank you, Dr. Schneider. Would three o'clock next Wednesday be a good time for you to come? Mrs. Bearner is free at that time."

Caller: "I'll be there. Could you tell me exactly where you are located?"

You: "We're at the corner of French and Boulder, across from the concert hall. Can you find that?"

Caller: "All set. Thanks for your help."

You: "Thank you for calling, Dr. Schneider. We look forward to seeing you. Goodbye."

In the next five simulations, assume that you are a secretary for Monarch Information Systems. Make the outgoing calls that are simulated, and read the dialogue that follows.

Simulation 6 *You are asked to call Coventry Computers to inquire about an error on a recent bill. The following conversation takes place.*

You: "This is [*name*] of Monarch Information Systems. We seem to have a problem on our last statement. May I speak to someone in your billing department?"

Coventry Computers: "Thank you for calling. I'll connect you to Mary Ann Barrett, who will help you." Call is connected.

Coventry: "Mary Ann Barrett. May I help you?"

You: "Yes. This is [*name*] of Monarch Information Systems. Would you check our July statement to see if we were charged twice for the same software package? I believe an error was made."

Coventry: "If that is the case, I apologize. May I review it and get right back to you?"

You: "That would be fine. My number is (555) 294-6181. When can I expect to hear from you?"

Coventry: "I'll get back to you within fifteen minutes. Is that okay?"

You: "Yes, it is. Thank you."

Simulation 7 *You are asked to call for information about office furniture your supervisor wishes to purchase. The following conversation takes place.*

Rogers Office Supply: "This is Bob Worth speaking. May I help you?"

You: "This is [*name*] of Monarch Information Systems. We're interested in buying furniture for our office. Specifically, we need a secretarial workstation, an executive desk, a conference table, and four chairs. Do you have a catalogue?"

Rogers: "Yes, we do. Our catalogues offer a broad selection of choices and price ranges."

You: "Sounds good. Please send that to my attention at 100 Plaza Center here in the city. When may I expect it?"

Rogers: "You'll have it by Friday. Thank you."

Simulation 8 *You are asked to call an executive of another company to deliver a message from your supervisor.*

You: "This is [*name*] of Monarch Information Systems. I would like to leave a message for Mr. Hart from Ms. Borden."

Mr. Hart's Assistant: "Certainly. I'll be happy to give Mr. Hart the message."

You: "Thank you. Ms. Borden wishes to reschedule tomorrow morning's appointment to a later date. She apologizes, but her mother is being operated on in the morning, and Ms. Borden wishes to be there. She'll call Mr. Hart tomorrow afternoon to reschedule."

Assistant: "I'll see that Mr. Hart gets the message. Thank you."

Simulation 9 *You are asked to call an applicant for a position to tell her she should come in for an interview.*

You:	"Hello, Ms. Bevans? This is [*name*] of Monarch Information Systems. You recently submitted a resume in response to our ad in *The New York Times,* and I'm calling to set up an interview."
Ms. Bevans:	"That's good news. I can make myself available whenever you wish."
You:	"Ms. Borden asked if you would come in Thursday morning at one o'clock. Would that be a good time?"
Ms. Bevans:	"I'll be there."
You:	"Do you know how to get to our office? We're on the second floor of the Dart Building in Room 509."
Ms. Bevans:	"Yes, I can find it. See you Thursday. Thank you."

Simulation 10   *You are asked to call the local Rotary Club president about the length and timing of a speech your supervisor is scheduled to make at a Rotary luncheon.*

You:	"Hello, Mr. Porter. This is [*name*] of Monarch Information Systems, Nancy Borden's assistant. Ms. Borden is speaking at your meeting next Tuesday. She asked me to call to find out what time she's scheduled to speak and how much time she has. Do you have that information?"
Rotary Club President:	"I sure do. Nancy is scheduled to speak from 12:45 to 1:00 P.M. We are looking forward to her talk."
You:	"I'll tell her that. Thanks for the information."

TELEPHONE VOICE EVALUATION

Speaker: _____

Date: _____

Evaluated by: _____

	WEAK	FAIR	SATISFACTORY	GOOD	VERY GOOD
1. Tone of Voice:					
2. Warmth:					
3. Clarity:					
4. Enthusiasm:					
5. Inflection:					
6. Confidence:					
7. Sincerity:					
8. Volume:					
9. Enunciation:					
10. Pace:					

COMMENTS:

MAJOR STRENGTH(S):

AREAS THAT NEED IMPROVEMENT:

Your instructor may evaluate your voice and/or have your classmates do so. Otherwise, you may tape your own voice and provide your own self-evaluation.

Additional critique forms are provided in the Appendix.

5.4   IMPROVING YOUR TELEPHONE VOICE

The purpose of the simulated telephone conversations is to provide you with a diagnostic tool to help you evaluate your telephone voice. The feedback of your instructor, your classmates, or even your own self-evaluation should point out your strengths as well as those areas you need to improve. Once you have this information, you need to do certain things to improve, to bring about CHANGE, to make your telephone voice more professional.

Start by noting on the evaluation sheets the voice characteristics on which you were ranked Good or Very Good. Consider your strong points and make a conscious decision to continue doing whatever you are doing that received a favorable evaluation. Pay attention to the comments of your instructor and/or classmates.

Next, focus on those characteristics ranked Satisfactory or lower and compare those evaluations to the comments under Areas That Need Improvement. These are the areas you will have to concentrate on in order to be more professional. Following are some suggestions on things to check or do for each voice characteristic evaluated.

If You Need to Improve	Try
Tone of Voice	Listening to yourself on a tape recorder. Experiment with changed delivery until you are pleased. Listen to recordings of the speeches of John F. Kennedy or Martin Luther King, Jr., so that you have role models. If you work in an office, listen to experienced professionals use the telephone. Learn by imitation.
Warmth	Checking your PMA (Positive Mental Attitude). Warmth is hard to fake. You have to feel it to project it.
Clarity	Reading from a book or favorite poem. Tape-record your reading. Now do the same reading, emphasizing all *p, t, d, k, b, l, th, ch, sh,* and *sch* sounds. Listen to the second recording, and you will hear how much clearer you sound.
Enthusiasm	Checking your nonverbal behavior. If you are slumped in a chair and have a bored expression on your face, it is difficult to sound enthusiastic. Once again, PMA comes into play.
Inflection	Listening to yourself on a tape recorder, with particular emphasis on imitating experienced professionals.
Confidence	Checking your own self-image. If you feel good about yourself and what you are doing, it will come across.
Sincerity	Asking yourself whether you are genuinely other-oriented, and whether you care about doing your best.

If You Need to Improve	Try
Volume	Practicing at home to lower or increase the volume, whichever is needed. Often, just an awareness of how you sound is enough to bring about change.
Enunciation	Reading aloud, emphasizing the consonant sounds listed under the third characteristic. Also, talking more slowly may help this problem.
Pace	Using models to imitate as was suggested for the first characteristic. Find the middle ground, a pace that is comfortable for you and the listener, and vary it with content.

The vast majority of people are able to improve with practice and feedback. Some people who have greater problems to overcome, may have to take a speech course or work with a speech therapist.

5.5   CHOOSING YOUR WORDS AND PHRASES WELL

Developing a professional telephone voice is only part of your task. In chapter 2 you learned that the words and phrases you use in telephone transactions *are more important* than they are in face-to-face encounters. The primary reason for this is that nonverbal communication such as facial expressions, eye contact, and body posture are not at work. While it is difficult to be certain of the relative impact of voice and words, an educated guess might be 60 percent vocal and 40 percent verbal. Having already focused on acquiring a pleasing telephone voice, you must turn now to the verbal part of telephone communication.

A current bumper sticker reads, "BE ODD, BE COURTEOUS." The implication is that the courteous driver is the exception in a time when basic etiquette is a rarity. In business telephone communication, however, courtesy is the cardinal rule. It should be your starting point as you begin to consider what you are going to say in telephone conversations.

Sandra Henselmeier, president of Better Business Communications, a training and development consulting firm, stresses courtesy as the key to telephone communication.

The following simple—but magic—words and phrases create and maintain a positive company image:

"Please."

"Thank you."

"May I help you?"

"May I put you on hold?"

"May I transfer you?"

Make these expressions the cornerstone of your telephone vocabulary and you can be certain you are on solid ground. They create a caring, other-oriented impression that is sure to trigger a favorable response from the other party.

Another way to let the other party know that he/she is important to you is to use his/her name several times during the conversation. This is not only a compliment, but it personalizes the exchange. Don't, however, use first names unless a friendly relationship between you and the other party has been established over a period of time. When in doubt, use the full name.

"Thank you for calling, Ms. Archer, I will give your message to Mr. Bolt, and you can expect to hear from him tomorrow morning."

Also, develop the habit of using titles when you address others. People have earned the right to a professional title by education, experience, or accomplishment, and it is correct to acknowledge their status. It never hurts to make others feel important.

"Nice to hear from you, Doctor Kendall. Just one moment and I'll connect you."

"I have a message for you, Professor Ponte."

In addition to being courteous, you must observe the basic principles of language usage if you wish to create positive impressions. Here are some of them.

1. Use words that you are comfortable with, those that are part of your "natural" vocabulary. Don't try to impress others with obscure five-syllable words. Consider your listener and use language that will best communicate the message.
2. Be concise and get to the point. In business, time is valuable and cannot be wasted with wordiness.
3. Be wary of turning your dialogue into a babble of jargon. In today's computerized, high-tech world, there is real danger that meaning may be lost in a clutter of technical terms and acronyms. If your listener is not familiar with the jargon you use, you must provide clear explanations.
4. Remember the statement made in chapter 1 that most business telephone conversations are formal transactions. As such, slang and overly casual cliches that are acceptable in informal interchanges are not appropriate and should be avoided.

Since the next three sections in this chapter discuss ways to begin and end telephone conversations as well as the need to use positive language, we will conclude this section by listing phrases to use in situations that occur commonly in the body of phone conversations. It is important to note here that some situations occur so frequently in telephone communication that it is helpful to develop standard responses appropriate to each situation.

Situation	Response
Connecting a caller.	"Yes, just one moment and I'll connect you."
Unable to connect a caller because party called is on another line.	"Mr. Landry has another call right now. May I put you on hold or would you like Mr. Landry to return your call?"
Unable to connect because party called is not in.	"Ms. Cooper is not in the office at the moment. May I take a message?"
	"Mr. Loomis is out of town this week. Is there something I could help you with?"
	"Ms. Harper is not in the office today, but she'll be calling in this afternoon. May I give her a message?"
When party calling has the wrong department.	"The Student Activities department handles yearbook distribution; Wait one moment and I'll transfer your call."
When you don't know the party calling.	"... and your name is?"
When you want to know the purpose of an in-coming call.	"... and the reason for your call is?"

5.6   ANSWERING CALLS AND PLACING CALLS

In chapter 1 you learned that many people with whom you speak form their impressions of your company, its products, and services, by the way you present yourself to them on the phone. This is such an important point, it cannot be overemphasized. Now we can add that the most crucial part of the phone conversation contributing to that impression is the first part—what you say when you answer the phone or how you initiate communication by placing a call. In both instances, first impressions are lasting impressions and often influence the quality of the communication that follows.

Knowing this, you should form habits of answering calls that you can repeat over and over, confident that you are making a positive first impression. Prepare to make such an impression by putting aside whatever you are doing and direct your total attention to the incoming call. Do not let the first sounds a caller hears be the last words of a conversation you were having. Adopt a PMA (Positive Mental Attitude) and be ready to sound friendly and cheerful. Pick up the phone any time between the first and second ring whenever possible. Allowing too many unnecessary rings is unbusinesslike.

What you actually say when answering calls will depend on a few variables. Many companies have definite preferences as to how they wish incoming calls handled and will so instruct new employees. For example, companies wishing to create a warm, personable image may tell employees to identify themselves by their first names only. Apart from these special instructions, responses to incoming calls will generally follow certain patterns and depend on your position in the company. Here are the most common patterns.

1. If your line is the first contact that a caller has with your firm (e.g., you are a receptionist or switchboard operator), you should identify your company and then yourself:

   "Mitchell Building Company, Bob Wren speaking."

2. If your office may have calls transferred to it or may be dialed directly, you would answer this way:

   "Engineering Department, Bob Wren speaking."

3. If you are a secretary or administrative assistant to another person, answer this way:

   "Betty Ward's office, Bob Wren speaking. May I help you?"

Perhaps the most disconcerting thing to a business caller is to get a busy signal. Business phones are not supposed to be busy. We expect companies to have enough lines to handle large numbers of incoming calls. In October 1987, when the stock market crashed, many customers got constant busy signals when they tried to phone their stock brokers. As a result brokers lost customers to other brokers, and some customers quit trading stocks altogether. Guard against this by keeping your lines as free as possible. In particular, don't make long personal calls. Learn how multibutton telephones work so you may handle simultaneous incoming calls. Don't panic or rush. Give each call the time and attention it deserves.

You already have learned that business people should place their own telephone calls, even long-distance calls. It is simply the most efficient way. You also know how important it is to plan your call before you make it. You even know that the best time to place calls is in the mornings from Tuesday to Friday. These are useful strategies, but we are concerned here with what to say when you place calls.

One habit you need to form is to identify yourself as soon as the other phone is answered. Always, no exceptions.

"Good afternoon, this is Ron Brown with Morris Metals. May I speak with Joyce Adams, please?"

When you are connected to the person you are calling, you should identify yourself again unless you are on a friendly basis and know your voice will be recognized. If in doubt, identify yourself. Next, ask the person if he/she has time to speak with you. The conversation might sound like this:

"Joyce Adams speaking."

"Good afternoon, This is Ron Brown with Morris Metals. How are you today?"

"I'm fine, Ron. Nice to hear from you."

"Joyce, do you have a few minutes now to discuss your recent order?"

Notice that the social amenities are brief, and the caller wastes no time in stating the purpose of the call. Again, a proper beginning sets the stage for a productive exchange.

5.7 ENDING TELEPHONE CONVERSATIONS

A more difficult verbal challenge to master is learning how to conclude phone conversations tactfully without offending the other person. As you consider this problem, two communication principles seem to be in conflict:

1. Remember, the cardinal rule of telephone communication is courtesy. This means you must always be mindful of the feelings of the other party.
2. At the same time that you are stressing courtesy, you must also be assertive and protect your own interests. In this case, you are trying to protect your business time.

Courteous assertiveness, a combination of the two communication principles, provides the answer. When the business of the call is completed and it is time to go on to other work, initiate the end of the call yourself whenever possible. That is being assertive; But do it tactfully by indicating the time to conclude has come. You can do this by expressing your appreciation of the other person's time and attention. That is being courteous.

"I don't want to take up any more of your time. Thanks for being so helpful."

"It was a pleasure talking with you, Mr. Burns. I hope to meet you in person soon."

"You have answered all my questions, Judy. I'll see you Tuesday morning."

If the other person is long-winded and persists in continuing the conversation, you may have to be more forceful.

"Jack, I have to go now. It was nice talking to you."

"Mrs. Brown, I have a client waiting to see me. May we continue this conversation another time?"

"I have to leave for an appointment now. Thanks again for the information."

These are all acceptable ways to end phone calls. They are both courteous and firm. As such, the last impression you leave will be a friendly, businesslike one. One last word. Disconnect by depressing the button, rather than replacing the receiver. Otherwise, you risk the sound of a slammed receiver.

5.8 USING POSITIVE LANGUAGE

You have been encouraged to adopt a Positive Mental Attitude prior to making or receiving calls. One of the keys to PMA is the use of positive language—words that people like. Upbeat words, words with positive connotations, create the right psychological tone in which productive communication thrives. The opposite happens when negative words are used and a climate of negativism results.

Corporations have known this truth about language for years and have encouraged employees to use positive words in their communications with customers and the public. Check the lists of words people like and dislike (below) to see if your present phone vocabulary is positive enough. If it is not, start to change now.

Words People Like

ability	distinction	initiative	recommend
achieve	economy	integrity	reliable
advance	effective	intelligence	responsible
appreciate	efficient	kind	service
approval	energy	loyalty	stability
benefit	enthusiasm	majority	success
capable	excellence	merit	superior
cheer	faith	notable	thorough
commendable	genuine	opportunity	thoughtful
concentration	grateful	please	truth
confidence	guarantee	practical	valuable
conscientious	harmonious	prestige	vital
cooperation	helpful	progress	wisdom
courtesy	honesty	reasonable	you
dependable	improvement	recognition	yours

Words People Dislike

abandoned	evict	lazy	standstill
abuse	failure	long-winded	stunted
alibi	fault	meager	stupid
allege	fear	misfortune	superficial
beware	flagrant	negligence	tamper
blame	flimsy	obstinate	tardy
cheap	fraud	opinionated	timid
commonplace	gloss over	prejudiced	unfair
crooked	harp upon	pretentious	unfortunate
deadlock	ignorant	retrench	unsuccessful
decline	illiterate	rude	untimely
desert	implicate	shrink	waste
disaster	impossible	slack	weak
discredit	insolvent	squander	worry
dispute	in vain	stagnant	wrong

Develop the habit of stressing that which is positive in a situation. Listen to the following statements, and contrast them with those that follow. Which are more hopeful, more productive sounding?

1. a. "I can have the market survey to you by next Friday."
   b. "I won't be able to get that market survey to you until next Friday."
2. a. "I will have to check with marketing on your question and get back to you with an answer."

       b. "I don't know anything about that situation."

  3. a. "We are confident that the job will be finished on time."

       b. "You don't have to worry about any failure on our part."

  4. a. "We have enough faith in your company to know that any delays were unavoidable."

       b. "I don't want to hear any alibis."

  5. a. "Here is what I can do."

       b. "I can't do that."

  6. a. "And the spelling of your name is?"

       b. "Can you spell your name for me?"

  7. a. "I am waiting for a decision."

       b. "They won't approve that."

  8. a. "I am the accounting department's secretary."

       b. "You have the wrong department."

  9. a. "We'll do our best to get the job done."

       b. "We may not be able to finish the job.

10. a. "The truth of the situation is . . . ."

       b. "I'm going to level with you."

5.9 PRACTICING YOUR TELEPHONE RESPONSES

Just as you had to practice and evaluate your telephone voice in order to be professional, so too must you practice the words and phrases that are effective in telephone communication. The difference in the simulated exercises that follow is that you must provide the words. There are no scripts, only brief descriptions of a business situation in which you must play a role.

Write your responses in the space provided and be prepared to read your responses aloud should your instructor ask. How you use the exercises will depend on whether other roles are assigned to classmates. Before beginning these exercises you may wish to review sections 5.4–5.7 in this chapter.

PRACTICE

EXERCISES

Simulated Telephone Situations

Simulation 1 *As the switchboard operator at Fenwick Badge Company you encounter the following situations:*

1. You are unable to connect an incoming call for Mr. Mason because he is not in.

_____

_____

_____

_____

_____

2. You are unable to connect an incoming call for Mr. Mason because he is on another line.

_____

_____

_____

_____

_____

3. You wish to know the name of the party calling before you connect.

_____

_____

_____

_____

_____

4. You wish to know the purpose of an incoming call before you connect.

_____

_____

_____

_____

_____

Simulation 2   1. You are the switchboard operator at Parker Films. All incoming calls come to you. How would you answer the telephone?

_____

_____

_____

_____

_____

2. You are an administrative assistant to Mary White, vice president of the sales department, at Parker Films. How would you answer the telephone?

_____

_____

_____

_____

_____

3. You are an office assistant in the advertising department at Parker Films. A call for the sales department is incorrectly connected to your phone. How would you handle the situation?

_____

_____

_____

_____

_____

4. You are an administrative assistant at Parker Films. You are calling Jane Norton to discuss new films that will be ready for distribution soon. The discussion will take a little while. How would you start the call?

_____

_____

_____

_____

_____

Simulation 3

1. As an administrative assistant at Parker Films, you have called Jane Norton. Your business is completed, and you wish to end the call. What are two possible ways to end the call?

a. _____

_____

_____

b. _____

_____

_____

2. Jane Norton persists in continuing the conversation long after business is finished. What are two more forceful ways to conclude the call?

a. _____

_____

_____

b. _____

_____

_____

Simulation 4   *Reword the following statements so they have a more positive psychological impact.*

1. "I don't know anything about it. That's not my department."

   _____

   _____

   _____

2. "We can't deliver those parts until next week."

   _____

   _____

   _____

3. "I can't get that approved."

   _____

   _____

   _____

4. "Don't start giving me excuses."

   _____

   _____

   _____

5. "We don't stock that product."

   _____

   _____

   _____

ASSIGNMENTS FOR CHAPTER 5

1. List five personality traits you would like your telephone voice to communicate.

2. Discuss the environmental factors that have played a role in shaping your present telephone voice.

3. As a result of the simulated telephone conversations you read, what changes in your telephone voice are you trying to make? Discuss.

4. Discuss what is meant by "courteous assertiveness." Cite an example of a situation in which you might have to be courteously assertive.

5. Without referring to the lists provided in this chapter, write ten words that people like and ten words that people dislike.

6. Write a short definition of the following key words and phrases from chapter 5.

Attitude change

Enunciation

Rapport

Pace

First impressions

▶ REVIEW QUIZ FOR CHAPTER 5

Indicate whether the following statements are true or false by circling your answer.

1. According to Ralph Proodian, the standard telephone may transmit messages to the listener that the speaker does not intend.

True   *False*

2. Your telephone voice results entirely from your biological makeup.

True   *False*

3. In order to approximate your natural speaking voice, hold the mouthpiece about four inches from your mouth.

True   *False*

4. Today's telephones carry your voice at the speed of light.

True   *False*

5. The average speaker talks at a rate of 125–250 words per minute.

True   *False*

6. The most critical part of the phone conversation that contributes to a positive or negative impression is the first part.

True   *False*

7. You should form habits of answering calls in the same way.

True   *False*

8. During the stock market crash of October 1987, many customers were not able to reach their stock brokers by phone.

True   *False*

9. You should allow the other party to initiate the end of a phone conversation.

True   *False*

10. The cardinal rule of telephone communication is courtesy.

True   *False*

Telephone Strategies That Work

Learning Objectives

At the completion of this chapter, you will be able to

- Schedule second calls in order to increase chances of completing calls and minimizing "telephone tag."

- Take clear and complete phone messages.

- Develop cost-saving habits that will use the business telephone in the most economical ways.

- Place callers on hold and transfer incoming calls in the most courteous and efficient manner.

- Screen incoming calls for three different business situations.

- Use strategies in order to penetrate screens and successfully complete more calls.

6.1 SCHEDULING CALLS TO PREVENT TELEPHONE TAG

Telephone tag is the plague of the busy business executive. It is so named because too many people spend too much time trying and failing to reach (catch) each other by phone. When one person is unable to contact another, a message is usually left, asking for the call to be returned. This begins the process (game of tag) all over again. Theoretically, the game can go on forever without the two people reaching each other. Judging by the 75 percent rate of failure of first calls to reach their intended party, telephone tag is epidemic and a major time-waster. How big a time-waster is it? According to AT&T the average business person who attempts thirty calls a day completes only eight of them on the first try, and then spends additional hours each week trying to complete the other twenty-two calls.

Mark McCormack offers a solution to this persistent problem. He suggests that, instead of asking to have a call returned, you might ask when the other person will be available and place the second call yourself at that time. While this method may work for McCormack, it seems to have specific limitations. For instance, if the person you are trying to reach is traveling, communication may not take place for an unacceptable period of time.

Instead, try this three-step approach which is sure to cut down on telephone tag:

1. Make most of your calls (or encourage your supervisor to do so) in the mornings from Tuesday through Friday. As you know, research shows more calls are completed at these times. Scheduling a half-hour or an hour for telephone calls is efficient time management. Make a list of calls according to their relative importance and work your way through the list, checking off the completed calls.

2. If your call is not completed on the first try, use the McCormack suggestion and ask when you can call back. But don't stop there. Offer the other option of having the call returned by indicating exactly when you will be able to receive a call. The key to success is to set specific times and to avoid vague statements.

   SPECIFIC: "I will call Ms. Burson back tomorrow morning at 10:00 A.M."
   VAGUE: "Would you have Ms. Burson return my call?"

3. If Steps 1 and 2 fail, you may conclude that you are being avoided. When that happens, it is time to write a business letter, which you can mail or fax.

PRACTICE EXERCISES

Simulated Telephone Situations

Just as you did in the exercises in chapter 5, write your response in the space provided and be prepared to read the response aloud should your instructor call on you.

Simulation Set 1

1. You are attempting to call Mr. Harold of Benton Bookstores. He is not in the office. What would you say and do in order to increase the chances of completing the second call?

_____

_____

_____

_____

_____

_____

_____

_____

_____

2. You are trying to reach Ms. Gloria Master of National Advertising. She is traveling and will be out of her office for a week. She calls in daily for messages. You need to talk to her in the next two days. What would you say and do in order to reach her on time?

_____

_____

_____

_____

_____

_____

_____

_____

_____

| 6.2 | **TAKING TELEPHONE MESSAGES** |

If you work in any capacity in a business office, chances are you will be answering phones for people who are not there. You may have to do this often as a regular part of your job, or it may happen infrequently. Regardless of how often you take messages for another party, you must always do so in a precise and professional manner. Taking clear messages that contain complete information marks you as someone who cares about the total organization's welfare. Taking sloppy, incomplete messages suggests you are concerned solely with your own affairs and have little respect for the needs of others.

It is important not to underestimate this aspect of telephone communications. You already know that 75 percent of business calls are not completed on the first call. It follows that messages will have to be taken for these calls. The quality of the message taken will often determine how productive the next step in communication is. Follow this golden rule and you will do fine:

Take phone messages for others as you would like to have them taken for you when you are away from your desk.

Most businesses provide standard forms similar to the ones shown on page 66. Though the forms may differ slightly in detail, they all must contain essential facts. The person receiving the message must be able to learn these things at a glance:

1. The name of the caller along with his/her title and company name, if available.
2. The date and time of the call.
3. The complete phone number of the caller.
4. The message, presented clearly and concisely.
5. The name of the person who took the message.

Each of these items is equally necessary to a complete message. The most common problems with phone messages in business offices are that they are either incomplete or illegible. To protect against both of these pitfalls, you need to take your time with the caller to obtain total information. Ask questions and repeat names and numbers to be certain they are correct. Above all else, *write or print the message clearly*. Too many business messages are written hurriedly and illegibly. A complete message is of little use if it cannot be read. When in doubt, PRINT. Some telephone communication advisors suggest that messages should go beyond the basic facts of a call. They advise the message taker to characterize the emotions of the caller and to comment on any other general impressions. While this may be all right for a secretary or administrative assistant who has come to know customers or clients and the nature of particular business relationships, it may also be a risky tactic that could lead to mistakes or misunderstandings. Until your experience allows for more subjective interpretations of calls, stick to the facts when taking messages.

Simulation Set 2

1. Contrast the two types of messages shown on page 66. The first is more professional in all respects. The second is less satisfactory. List the problems with the second message and explain how it could be improved.

_____

_____

_____

_____

_____

2. As a secretary at Harrison Publishing, you have answered Mr. Phil Gray's phone while he is at lunch. The caller is Linda Hopkins of Central Community College. She wishes to speak to Mr. Gray about a new science textbook, *Exploring the Universe*. She wants Mr. Gray to call her back after 3:00 P.M. on Tuesday of the same week. Her number is 264-3722. Fill out the blank message form for Mr. Gray as shown on page 67.

6.3 CUTTING TELEPHONE COSTS

As technology has improved over the years, the telephone is being used more and more to transact business. Because of this increased usage, the

<table>
<tr><td>

To _Mr. Wehby_

Date _7/18_   Time _1:40_   (P.M.)

WHILE YOU WERE OUT

Ms _Jane Beamer_

of _Newport Systems_

Phone _401_ _789-6200_ _158_
    Area Code   Number   Extension

TELEPHONED	X	PLEASE CALL	X
CALLED TO SEE YOU		WILL CALL AGAIN	
WANTS TO SEE YOU		RUSH	
		RETURNED YOUR CALL	

Message _Is interested in learning more about our direct mail marketing programs._

Tina R.
Operator

</td><td>

To _Ms. Panduquet_

Date _8/2_   Time

WHILE YOU WERE OUT

M _Billy_

of _Timing Services_

Phone _241-3677_
    Area Code   Number   Extension

TELEPHONED	X	PLEASE CALL	
CALLED TO SEE YOU		WILL CALL AGAIN	
WANTS TO SEE YOU		RUSH	X
		RETURNED YOUR CALL	

Message _Emergency_

_RJ_
Operator

</td></tr>
</table>

cost of telephone service is now a major business expense for most companies. Budget-conscious companies try to control telephone costs just as they do any other significant expense item. As a conscientious employee, you can contribute to that effort by using your business telephone in the most efficient and economical ways.

You can start by developing these cost-saving habits:

1. *Keep personal calls to a minimum.*
   This has been mentioned earlier in a discussion of time-wasting behaviors. What needs to be mentioned now is that personal calls cost money, particularly if you are calling long-distance. Many businesses have the phone company separate toll call charges by the phones they were made from and then bill the employee. This can be embarrassing, expensive, and damaging to an employee who has made too many calls.

2. *Take phone companies' suggestions to do the following:*
   a. Ask for credit when you are connected to a wrong number.
   b. Ask for credit when your connection is so poor that communication is impossible.
   If you don't ask for credit in these situations, your company is, in effect, paying for services you didn't receive.

3. *Use special directories such as the **AT&T Toll-Free 800 Directory.***
   Many businesses around the country have been provided with 800 numbers for business use, and the potential for savings to the customer is considerable. If, for example, you are given the responsibility of making travel arrangements for other employees, you can generally call airlines, hotels, and auto rental agencies without charge in order to purchase tickets or make reservations.

```
To _____
                                              A.M.
Date _____  Time _____  P.M.

         WHILE YOU WERE OUT

M _____

of _____

Phone _____
        Area Code      Number      Extension
```

TELEPHONED		PLEASE CALL	
CALLED TO SEE YOU		WILL CALL AGAIN	
WANTS TO SEE YOU		RUSH	
	RETURNED YOUR CALL		

```
Message _____

_____

_____

_____

                        _____
                             Operator
```

An 800 number can be dialed direct just like any other call. Simply dial "1" (in most states) followed by the number. For 800 Directory Assistance, dial 1-800-555-1212. When you call 800 numbers, be prepared by having close at hand all the information, questions, credit-card numbers, and anything else necessary to do business. Employees who are sincere about cutting costs will familiarize themselves with the 800 Directories and use them whenever possible.

4. *Use telephone directories rather than incur the information charges of using directory assistance.*
   If you make frequent calls to other cities and states, you should obtain directories for those locations.

5. *If you make any long-distance business calls, be sure you are doing so in the most economical way.*
   Long-distance phone calls are so common in today's business world that we need to spend more time considering how best to make them. The

least expensive long-distance method is **direct dialing,** which is done easily by dialing 1 + area code and the seven-digit number. To do this, you need to know the number, which, if it is one you call frequently, should be readily available in a list of commonly called numbers. If you do not know the number of the business you are calling, dial 1 + area code and 555-1212, which will connect you with information in the area you are calling. Should you be calling across time zones, you need to be certain that the business you are calling will be open. Most telephone directories have a map (see figure on page 69) showing area codes and **time zones** throughout the United States. Use them as long as you need them to save both time and money. You may also dial foreign countries directly and economize. Codes for foreign countries can also be found in most telephone directories.

Simulation Set 3

1. Obtain an *AT&T Toll-Free 800 Directory*. Using it, look up the numbers of any five major airlines, auto rental agencies, and hotels.

Airlines	Name	Numbers

Auto Rental Agencies	Names	Numbers

Hotel Chains	Names	Numbers

2. In order to avoid making expensive long-distance calls at the wrong times across time zones, you need to familiarize yourself with time zone differentials. Assume you are calling from New York and wish to reach another company at 10:00 A.M., their time. What time would you have to place the call if the company was located in:

TIME ZONE AND PHONE AREA CODES

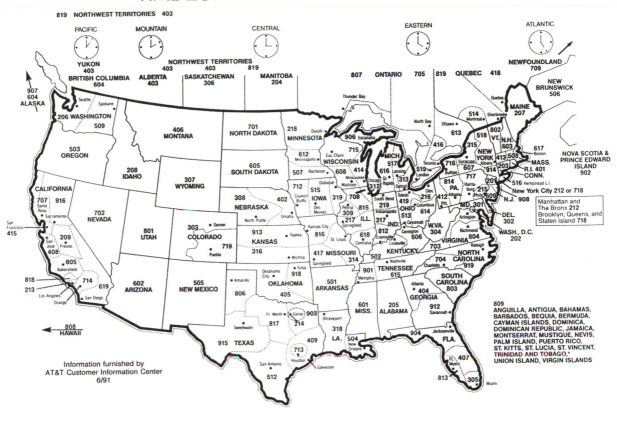

Information furnished by
AT&T Customer Information Center
6/91

State	Time
Wichita, Kansas	_____
Atlanta, Georgia	_____
Spokane, Washington	_____
Chicago, Illinois	_____
South Bend, Indiana	_____
Phoenix, Arizona	_____

6.4   PUTTING CALLS ON HOLD AND TRANSFERRING CALLS

There are many occasions when you have to ask callers to wait or hold while you attend to another duty. You might have to answer another incoming call or obtain information for the caller, or you may be screening the call for your supervisor. Whatever the reason, you must handle the situation correctly to avoid irritating the caller. Follow these steps, and you should get a favorable response.

1. Ask if you may place the caller on hold before you do it. You have no way of knowing whether this will be acceptable to the caller or not.

"May I put you on hold, please? I need to check the files for that information."

If you need to be away from the conversation for more than half a minute, return and ask if the caller wishes to remain on hold. Continue to do this in the event of an extended delay.

"Are you able to continue holding?"

2. When you are able to return, reestablish the tone of the communication.

"Mr. Dunham, thank you for being so patient. I have the information you need."

Sometimes you need to transfer calls within your company. This happens often when the caller requires information or service that you or your supervisor cannot provide. Again, not only do you need to know how to use the telephone equipment properly to transfer calls but, equally important, you need to manage the potentially annoying situation smoothly. Some basic steps serve as guidelines.

1. Explain the reason for the transfer to the caller.

"Ms. Jones, I am transferring your call to Bill Bartell in our public relations department. He should be able to help you."

2. Before you transfer the call, ask for the caller's name and telephone number in case the call is disconnected.

"Would you give a number at which you can be reached, Ms. Jones, in case we are disconnected?"

3. Before you transfer the call, give as much information as you are able to the person who will be receiving the call. This saves repetition and creates the possibility of a more productive exchange.

"Mr. Bartell, I have Ms. Jones on the line from *The Daily News.* She wants to talk to you about next week's convention."

Simulation Set 4

1. You are an administrative assistant for Oxford Insurance Company, working in the claims department. A policyholder, John Gibson, calls to inquire about a claim. It will take you a few minutes to get the information. What would you do and say to handle the call professionally?

_____

_____

_____

_____

_____

2. Working in the same position described above, you receive a call from a Mrs. Heller who wants to speak to someone in the sales department about buying an automobile policy. You have to transfer the call to Joan Penn in sales. What would you do and say to handle the call?

_____
_____
_____
_____
_____

6.5   SCREENING INCOMING CALLS

If you are a secretary or an administrative assistant, you may also be asked to screen incoming calls. This is a telephone task which is important since it serves your supervisor's needs. However, it is also a difficult situation which must be handled delicately and courteously to avoid offending the caller.

When you **screen** a telephone call, you are creating a protective barrier between the caller and your supervisor. It is your responsibility not to let anyone through the barrier until certain facts are established. You may also, in some instances, decide to keep the barrier up and not connect the caller.

Screening calls is an accepted business practice because it accomplishes several objectives. First, it conserves the time of busy people who cannot afford to have their work constantly interrupted. For example, an executive interviewing a prospective employee may decide not to accept calls out of courtesy to the person being interviewed.

In such a case, the screen will serve as an information-gathering technique resulting in a message to be acted upon at a later, more convenient time.

Administrative Assistant: "Good afternoon. Finch Products, Mary speaking. May I help you?"

Caller: "May I speak with Mr. Long, please?"

Administrative Assist.: "I'm sorry, Mr. Long is not available at the moment. Can someone else help you or may I take a message?"

Caller: "No, I need to talk to Mr. Long. This is Joan French of Henton Corporation calling. Would you have Mr. Long return my call? My number is 264-7722."

Administrative Assist.: "I will tell Mr. Long that you called, Ms. French. He can reach you at 264-7722; is that correct?"

A second reason for screening calls is to give your supervisor the opportunity to decide whether to receive the call or not. In fact, you may already have been told not to connect certain calls but, more often than not, that will be your supervisor's decision. This situation must be handled tactfully.

Secretary: "Good morning. Rapid Printing, Beth speaking. May I help you?"

Caller: "May I speak to Mr. Black, please?"

Secretary: "Just one moment, and I'll see if Mr. Black is available right now. May I ask who is calling?"

Caller: "This is Bob Bell of Hansom Delivery Services."

Now you contact Mr. Black to tell him Bob Bell is waiting. If he decides not to accept the call, you should handle it this way:

Secretary: "Thank you for waiting Mr. Bell. Mr. Black is in conference right now. Would you leave a number? I will ask him to return your call."

A final reason to screen calls is to provide your supervisor with sufficient information about the caller and the purpose of the call so that he or she may prepare to receive the call. Even though this preparation may just be a matter of seconds, it allows time to gather files that might be needed or to think about the call before answering.

Receptionist: "Good morning. Mary Johnson's office, Barbara speaking. May I help you?"

Caller: "May I speak with Ms. Johnson, please?"

Receptionist: "Certainly, may I tell her who is calling?"

Caller: "This is Professor Hurley."

Receptionist: "And the reason for your call is?"

Caller: "I wish to discuss my life insurance coverage with Ms. Johnson."

Receptionist: "Thank you. I'll connect you."

Asking about the purpose for the call can be easily misunderstood as being overly protective and should be discussed with your supervisor beforehand.

Screening must be understood for what it is, a time-saver and a support service for a busy executive. Occasionally, with aggressive, persistent callers, it requires assertiveness as well as tact. At other times, the screen will allow you to take care of routine matters without interrupting your supervisor. Remember to be courteous above all else.

Simulation Set 5

1. You have been told by your supervisor, Mr. Ryan, not to interrupt him for any reason. A call comes in from Mr. Quirk of Acme Corporation asking to speak to Mr. Ryan. What would you say to Mr. Quirk?

   _____

   _____

   _____

   _____

   _____

2. You are uncertain whether your supervisor, Mr. Ryan, wishes to receive a call from Ms. Kramer of Office Services. How would you handle the call if Mr. Ryan decides not to talk to Ms. Kramer at this time?

   _____

   _____

   _____

   _____

   _____

3. Mr. Ryan, your supervisor, has instructed you to obtain the name of any caller and the reason for the call before connecting him. A call comes in from a woman who does not identify herself. What would you say and do in this situation?

_____

_____

_____

_____

_____

6.6   GETTING THROUGH PROTECTIVE SCREENS

In the same way that you will use the screening techniques discussed in the previous section, you are sure to encounter similar barriers to calls you are trying to complete. Other switchboard operators, secretaries, or administrative assistants will be attempting to save their supervisor's time, obtain information from you, or block your call entirely. Knowing that this is an accepted business practice, you can expect screens and learn how to deal with them effectively.

Here are some ways to get through protective screens:

1. Call when the screens are down. Generally, this means calling before or after business hours or during lunch time.
2. Cultivate a friendly relationship with the person doing the screening. Be polite, get his/her name, and express thanks for any help you receive. You will be surprised at what other people will do for those who treat them with respect, courtesy, and warmth.
3. Make the job of the person doing the screening as easy as possible. Give full information as to your reason for calling and explain approximately how long your call will take.
4. If you get a time and date to call back, call the person doing the screening to remind them you will be calling at the agreed-upon time, and you anticipate being connected. Use this technique infrequently and only when other methods fail.

Simulation Set 6   1. As an administrative assistant at Power Systems, Inc., you run into a screen while trying to reach Dr. Burns of Northern County Hospital. What would you say and do to increase your chances of contacting Dr. Burns?

_____

_____

_____

_____

_____

_____

_____

_____

2. You have been told to call Dr. Burns back next Tuesday at 2:00 P.M. What might you do prior to that call? Include any dialogue.

_____

_____

_____

_____

_____

_____

_____

_____

_____

▶ ASSIGNMENTS FOR CHAPTER 6

1. List three steps you can take to minimize "telephone tag" and contact another party.

2. List all the information that should be included in a telephone message.

3. What are five ways to lower the cost of using a business telephone?

4. List three things to do when putting callers on hold.

5. List three reasons to justify the screening of incoming calls.

6. Write a short definition of these key words and phrases from chapter 6.

Telephone tag

Toll-Free 800 Directory

Time zones

Screening calls

Direct dialing

▶ REVIEW QUIZ FOR CHAPTER 6

Indicate whether the following statements are true or false by circling your answer.

1. Around 85 percent of telephone calls fail to reach their intended party on the first try.

True   _False_

2. Screening incoming calls is a commonly accepted business practice.

True   *False*

3. Screens sometimes allow supervisors to decide whether to receive calls or not.

True   *False*

4. Screens waste time by interrupting a more direct connection.

True   *False*

5. Screens may sometimes be penetrated by calling before normal business hours.

True   *False*

6. If you cultivate relationships with people who are screening for others, your chances of completing calls may be increased.

True   *False*

7. Clarity and completeness are the two most important qualities of phone messages.

True   *False*

8. Mark McCormack suggests that all callbacks should be scheduled.

True   *False*

9. Research shows phone calls are better completed in early afternoon, when people have returned from lunch.

True   *False*

10. Telephone costs may be cut by using direct dialing for long-distance calls.

True   *False*

CHAPTER

7

Challenging Telephone Situations

Learning Objectives

At the completion of this chapter, you will be able to

■ Explain why the business telephone is the most effective way to service customers.

■ Communicate with an angry caller in such a way as to convert the call into a calm, productive exchange.

■ Handle a complaint call so that a potential problem becomes an opportunity to strengthen customer relations.

■ Use the traditional five-step approach to selling that leads to effective telemarketing.

■ Collect overdue bills in an effective, yet tactful manner.

■ Cope with "telephone burnout" by using tested stress-reducing techniques that work.

7.1   SERVICING CUSTOMERS BY TELEPHONE

One AT&T television ad used to include the phrase, "The Business Telephone Is Your Business Lifeline." It was one phone company's way of saying that telephones are the most important way of connecting companies to their customers. While we can understand why a phone company wishes to emphasize the key role of the telephone in customer service, it is hard to disagree with that statement.

In a booklet entitled "Keeping Customers Satisfied," AT&T makes further claims that ring true in today's business world.

> A "phone in" customer service program effectively opens a two-way dialogue between you and the consumer. Your customer can learn about your product as you learn about their needs. Your friendly, knowledgeable customer service representative gives your company a personality, a decided advantage in the marketplace… . [I]t's a lot less expensive to keep a current customer satisfied than to acquire a new one. A responsive customer service program is the most cost-effective way to keep your customers happy and buying more.

There's more. The telephone is less expensive and faster than business correspondence as a means of satisfying customers. The telephone is, indeed, an effective business tool.

However, none of this comes easily. Whether you are a customer service representative or just an employee who occasionally deals with the public on the phone, it is virtually certain you will be confronted with challenges that will test your skills to the limit. This chapter is about being able to handle these challenges successfully. Whether the challenges come in the form of an angry caller, a complaining customer, or other stressful situations, there are techniques you can learn to deal with them.

A quality customer service program is the most cost-effective way to keep your customers happy.

7.2   SOOTHING THE ANGRY CALLER

It is not uncommon in business to have to deal with an emotional, angry person on the other end of the telephone. Often, this person can be hostile, even abusive, to you. The fact that you may not be responsible for the problem is not a factor. You are available—an easy target for frustrations. This situation is a potentially explosive one for, as we know, anger generally creates anger in return, and it is precisely this reaction you must avoid. Keep yourself calm and try these tactics:

1. Remind yourself that, regardless of what words are said, you should not take them personally. The anger is almost always directed at your organization and needs to be understood that way.
2. As you are listening, think of your objective—what you are trying to accomplish in this conversation. More often than not, you wish to solve a problem, and this needs to be done calmly and logically.
3. Defuse the caller's emotions by appealing to his or her rational self. An effective way to do that is to ask questions that require reasoned responses.

   "What can I do to help solve your problem, Mrs. Burke?" "Would a letter from me to your bank help?"

4. Correct the situation that is causing the anger or, if that is not possible, offer an explanation or alternative solution.

Although dealing with angry callers can be most unpleasant, it is a mark of **professionalism** to remain calm and courteous during such conversations.

PRACTICE EXERCISES

Simulated Telephone Situations

Once again, write your responses in the space provided and be prepared to read the response aloud should your instructor ask.

Simulation Set 1

1. You are a customer service representative for a major chain of department stores. A Mr. Bevans calls, furious about the fact that a VCR he purchased recently broke down while he was taping his favorite show. He is insulting and asks if you are any smarter than the "imbecile" who sold him the VCR. What would you do and say to handle the situation?

   _____

   _____

   _____

   _____

   _____

2. You are a customer service representative for a large discount brokerage firm. A Mr. Teir calls, angry because your phone has been busy and he was unable to sell shares of stock before the price dropped. What would you do and say to handle the situation?

_____

_____

_____

_____

_____

7.3   CAPITALIZING ON COMPLAINTS

Another potential problem is the complaint call. Complaining callers may or may not be angry and emotional, but they feel they have been wronged and they usually want you to set things right. A product has malfunctioned or an expected service hasn't been provided. Whatever the reason, or the cause, you are talking to an unhappy customer. The attitude that you bring to the complaint call is the critical point. If you approach complaints as unpleasant situations that have to be endured, your results will reflect that attitude. If, however, you take the view that a complaint call represents an opportunity to be capitalized on, an opportunity to keep an existing customer or even gain a new one, then the rewards you can reap will be substantial.

How substantial those rewards may be has been well documented by a study of Consumer Complaint Handling in America conducted by Technical Assistance Research Programs, Inc. (TARP). This study contends that the positive handling of complaints may, in fact, be the most effective way to build your customer confidence and referral business. Furthermore, the TARP study claims your most loyal customers are not those who have never had problems with your products, but buyers whose complaints were resolved satisfactorily. The study also found that many customers are hesitant about complaining to the manufacturer about product defects—although they pass the bad word to an average of nine or ten other people. They'll also gladly tell their friends—typically four or five of them—about their positive experiences with your company and its products.

Another benefit of paying close attention to complaining customers is that it is an invaluable source of feedback from the public. If you listen—really listen—you will pick up insights into consumer attitudes toward your company, its products, and the market in general. When patterns of consumer attitudes become apparent, you need to share that information with those in your organization who can take corrective measures.

Clearly then, the handling of complaints is something worth doing well. To be able to do so requires a systematic approach which, if followed step-by-step, will result in success. Follow these suggestions:

1. Don't think of a complaining caller as an opponent or adversary. Your attitude should be that you are there to help solve a problem that the caller has.
2. Listen well and take complete notes so that you have all the specific details on hand for quick reference.
3. If your company is wrong, apologize. Even if your company is not at fault, you can express regret so that the caller understands your concern.
4. Work toward a solution by identifying what the caller wishes to be done and what reasonably can be done. If necessary, offer alternatives and

be prepared to compromise. Remember that you wish to keep the customer for the future. Think long-term.

5. Be certain that you act on the problem immediately. When a solution is achieved, get back to the other party right away. Don't delay.

6. Let the caller know that he/she is a valued customer and you wish to keep him/her as a customer.

Handling complaints professionally requires careful use of language. Choose positive phrases that lead to solutions, and avoid defensive or antagonistic ones. Here are some statements to avoid:

"I just work here. There isn't anything I can do."

"Look, this is our company policy, and I can't do anything about it."

"I disagree with you completely."

"Do you understand what I just said?"

Instead, try statements like these:

"I understand just how you must feel."

"Perhaps we can find an alternative solution."

"What can we do to keep you as a customer?"

"Is there something else you might consider?"

Simulation Set 2

1. As a customer service representative for a major automobile company, you receive a call from Mr. Samson who claims to be a long-time buyer of your company's cars. His most recent purchase, however, is a lemon. There are a number of problems he mentions which his local dealer has not been able to correct. He threatens legal action. List the steps you would take on the telephone to resolve the conflict. What are some phrases you might use that would be helpful?

2. As a customer service representative for an office supply company, you get a call from a Mrs. Paul who has recently purchased two file cabinets

from your company. She claims that the locks on both cabinets have been broken. From her description, you conclude that she has inadvertently caused the problem by forcing the locks. Outline your strategy for resolving this complaint. Include statements or questions you might use that would be effective.

_____

_____

_____

_____

_____

_____

_____

_____

7.4 TELEMARKETING AND OTHER FORMS OF PERSUASION

More and more today, when the phone rings in American homes, the caller is a telemarketer trying to sell a product or service. If the caller is not attempting to sell directly, he/she may be taking a survey to get information to be used in a later marketing effort. This new reality, the use of the telephone as a major marketing tool, has created over two million jobs, and it is expected that, before the end of the century, eight million new positions in the field will be created. The extent of this rapid growth was described in a _Washington Monthly_ article:

> **Telemarketing**—the selling of goods and services over the phone may be the fastest growing industry in America. Banks, real-estate firms, stock brokerages, insurance companies, sporting-goods manufacturers, distributors, the arts, charities, politicians—nearly every group in the nation is on to the trend. Today an estimated 142,000 companies employ over two million telesales personnel who sell close to $200 billion in goods and service.

If you are employed as a telemarketer, it is possible that you will be given a written sales "script" to follow. Training will be provided, and as you become experienced, you will be able to move away from the script and personalize your sales effort. However, since all sales are essentially attempts at **persuasion,** you generally will be expected to follow the basic formula that has proved effective over time. Here is a five-step plan for selling effectively:

1. Introduce yourself and ask if you may have time to explain your purpose.
2. Explain your purpose.
3. Describe how the other person will benefit from your product or service.
4. Overcome objections and answer questions.
5. Ask for the business and end the call.

Telemarketing may be the fastest growing industry in the United States.

While this step-by-step approach may be an oversimplification, it is a fact that most sales calls, when analyzed, can be broken down to these five parts. A recent purchase made by my family serves to illustrate this point well.

A young woman from AT&T called one evening, introduced herself, and asked for a few minutes to talk about a new long-distance service. Since the amount of my long-distance charges had been a recent concern of mine, I agreed to listen. She explained how this new service could save my family a substantial amount of money each month. When I objected to the limited time in which calls could be made, she was ready with an alternative suggestion that was acceptable. She asked if I wished to take the plan and I agreed. Information was taken and the call ended. It was a classic, though relatively easy, sale.

Even if you are not involved in direct selling, chances are you will have to use the telephone to persuade someone. You may have to call outside to a municipal agency and convince the person you speak to that your company requires a particular service that is not being received. You may have to call a department head to suggest that a new piece of office equipment is needed. Whatever the situation, persuasion is just another type of selling and similar principles apply. Obviously, the most successful persuaders are those with pleasing personalities who project a positive attitude and who often get positive responses in return.

Simulation Set 3

1. You are a telemarketing representative for Norton Cable Television Company. Write down the steps you would take and the things you would say if you were trying to sign up new customers. Follow the five steps suggested in this section.

(1) _____

_____

_____

_____

(2) _____

_____

_____

_____

(3) _____

_____

_____

_____

(4) _____

_____

_____

_____

(5) _____

_____

_____

_____

2. You are looking for a position as a secretary-receptionist, and you are calling Ms. Burke of Pontiac Manufacturing for the purpose of obtaining an interview. What would you do and say in order to persuade Ms. Burke that you are someone worth seeing?

_____

_____

_____

_____

_____

_____

_____

_____

7.5   TELECOLLECTING

Of all the calls that people receive in their homes or businesses, calls from bill collectors are the least welcome. No one likes to be reminded that he or she is late to pay a bill or that credit is being jeopardized. However, as unwelcome as such calls may be, they are absolutely necessary to many businesses. As such, many jobs require employees to spend some or all of their time **telecollecting**—calling to persuade people to meet their financial obligations. It is not an easy task, and doing it well requires skill and tact.

Credit contributes to increased sales.

Successful telephone collectors understand the basic purpose of extending credit to customers. They realize that credit contributes to increased sales and that, whenever credit is given, there is a chance that some repayments will be late or not made at all. That is part of the risk of credit. The telephone collector's job is to maximize repayments without antagonizing the client who is a potential future customer. This dual responsibility is often difficult to keep balanced.

More often than not, telephone collection begins after regular billing or other written reminders have not generated a response. As a telecollector, you need to have full information on the history of the account being called. This will include past payment patterns, names of principals involved, details of transactions, and the degree of flexibility you can offer in each situation. Armed with complete information, make the call, identify yourself, and clearly state your purpose:

"We have not received a payment from you in three months, and I am calling to see if we can make the account current."

or

"I am calling about your bill, which is overdue."

Opening statements such as these will get a response from the customer. You must *listen* closely and assess what you hear. Depending on the nature of the response, you should request full payment or suggest an acceptable arrangement of partial payments.

"Are you able to pay the bill at this time?"

or

"Can you send half the amount due now and the balance by the first of next month?"

Once again, the actual situation will dictate your tactics. Some customers respond to appeals to pride and others need to be reminded that their credit standing may suffer. Whatever the exchange, you need to keep precise records of agreements that are reached so that later follow-ups can check to see if they were kept.

If you are given the job of collecting bills by phone, this does not mean you have the right to abuse or threaten people. Most states have laws regulating what phone collectors can and cannot do. Learn those laws and comply with them. Find out the limits on the frequency of calls and the hours of the day when calls can be made. Don't be antagonistic, as you will only get resentment in return. True, some customers will be more difficult than others, but that is the challenge. Remember the purpose of credit and think of yourself as a negotiator. Keep a positive attitude and try to come up with creative alternatives for the toughest cases. Slow payers have only a limited number of excuses they can present. Develop responses for each of these common excuses and, if you can't get a commitment for full payment, settle for a partial payment. Something is better than nothing.

Simulation Set 4

1. You are working in the credit department of the Williams Fuel Oil Company. You have to call James Lincoln, who owes your company $440 and has not made a payment in four months. It is January, the temperature is below freezing, and Mr. Lincoln had ordered another $150 of fuel oil. How would you handle the call?

_____

_____

_____

_____

_____

_____

_____

_____

_____

2. You are employed by Washington Financial Services, a company that specializes in auto loans. You have to call Betty Walsh whose payments on her 199– Ford are two months behind. What would you say in an effort to make the account current?

_____

_____

_____

_____

_____

_____

_____

_____

_____

_____

_____

7.6   PROTECTING AGAINST TELEPHONE BURNOUT

Telephone burnout is a reaction common to some office workers who spend much of their workday on the telephone. At its extreme, burnout is characterized by an inability to carry out telephone duties in a professional manner. Customer service representatives, telemarketers, and bill collectors are just a few of those who are potential candidates for burnout.

Burnout is usually caused by stress or, more precisely, an inability to cope with stress. Stress, on the other hand, may have a variety of causes. Causes of stress will vary with individuals, but some common ones are:

1. Personal problems brought into the office, e.g., financial difficulties or family tension.
2. Dissatisfaction with some aspect of a job such as salary or schedule.
3. Inability to get along with fellow workers.
4. A poor work environment.

Workers who spend most of their time on the telephone must learn to manage stress.

Regular exercise is one way to control stress.

5. Health problems.
6. An unfair workload, e.g., circuit overload for a switchboard operator.

Steven Danish, professor of preventive medicine at Virginia Commonwealth University defines *stress* as your body's response to any unusual demands made upon it. He explains further that all stress is not bad, and that a limited amount of stress may indeed improve your performance. Danish states that there are three general approaches to stress management: exercising regularly; learning to relax your body and mind; and changing your perceptions about your life situation and the way you deal with it.

Starting with these three general approaches, we can become much more specific in our efforts to deal with stress. For example, two of the physical problems that telephone workers suffer are lower back problems and frequent loss or cracking of their voices. To prevent lower back problems, you need to bring in cushions for proper back support if you are not provided with a proper chair. Take mini breaks and stretch your legs often, if only for a few seconds at a time. To minimize loss of voice, lubricate your throat with lukewarm water at regular intervals. Avoid cold drinks and any beverage with caffeine in it. Finally, don't smoke; smoking will only aggravate vocal problems caused by stress.

Usually, it is easier to manage the physical effects of stress than the psychological effects. Also, employees who are under psychological strain are often not able to communicate effectively by telephone. Their stress translates into short-tempered irritability, curt responses, and unpleasant exchanges. It is quite likely that the rude airline customer representative mentioned in chapter 1 (section 1.4) was a victim of stress. Clearly, this problem needs to be managed to prevent the likely result of lost business.

Because employee stress is such a real problem for businesses, Dr. Craig Mardus, stress consultant to corporations, created an innovative way to provide practical office stress education for employees who use the telephone frequently. Mardus, who calls his company "Stressbusters," designed stress pads, which combine a phone message pad with a stress tip for the office. The idea is to help people manage stress better and avoid burnout.

Here are nine suggestions from "Stressbusters:

1. Create some form of office support system. Use your coffee breaks to touch base with a co-worker you trust. Bounce around what's bothering you and get that person's opinion.
2. Be aware of your negative "self-talk." Most cases of job burnout have their little inner voices working overtime thinking negative thoughts.
3. Although losing yourself in your job can be very productive and increase your performance, make sure you don't lose an important part of yourself in the process.
4. To get through the stress of boring, daily routine, try personalizing your job. For example, discover your unique qualities such as patience, perseverance, or creativity. They will enable you to "shine" while doing your work, no matter how mundane.
5. When things start to go wrong at work, try not to take it personally, which lowers self-esteem while raising stress levels. Keep in mind that we all make mistakes, and that mistakes in no way affect our worth as a person.
6. Maintain a good sense of humor, which is essential for successful stress management. When we laugh, we release natural pain killers called endorphins into our bloodstreams.
7. Because office routine can be stressfully boring, vary your daily tasks, take creative lunch and coffee breaks, or have little contests with other employees on how to make the task less boring.
8. Since office rumors can be very stressful, take the time during the coffee breaks or staff meetings to set them straight. It will defuse the stress.
9. Personalize your workspace. Whether your workspace is a desk, an alcove, or an office, it should promote a sense of home and peace in order to be as stress-free as possible. Choose things from personal areas—hobbies, special interests, family photos, sports heroes, or art objects—to decorate your workspace. Make a statement about yourself that others will find revealing and personal.

Just being aware of stress-related burnout and ways to manage it can enable you to have a more satisfying and rewarding career. Try the above ideas and see if they work.

ASSIGNMENTS FOR CHAPTER 7

1. Explain the statement in the AT&T telephone ad, "The Business Telephone is Your Business Lifeline."

2. Explain one effective strategy to calm down an angry, emotional caller.

3. Discuss the findings of a study of Consumer Complaint Handling in America conducted by Technical Assistance Research Programs, Inc. (TARP).

4. List the five steps for effective selling discussed in this chapter.

5. Explain the basic purpose of extending credit to customers.

6. Write a short definition of these key words and phrases from chapter 7.

Professionalism

Telemarketing

Persuasion

Telecollecting

Telephone burnout

REVIEW QUIZ FOR CHAPTER 7

Indicate whether the following statements are true or false by circling your answer.

1. According to AT&T, it is more expensive to keep a customer satisfied than to acquire a new one.

    True   *False*

2. Business correspondence is less expensive than telephone communication.

    True   *False*

3. Anger often creates anger in return.

    True   *False*

4. Positive handling of complaints may lead to new customers.

    True   *False*

5. Telemarketing is a growth industry.

    True   *False*

6. Credit is a marketing strategy.

    True   *False*

7. Telephone collection calls are usually the first attempts to obtain payment.

    True   *False*

8. Many states have laws regulating what telephone collectors can do in their efforts to obtain payment.

    True   *False*

9. Causes of stress may vary from person to person.

    True   *False*

10. Some stress can be positive and contribute to improved performance.

    True   *False*

Appendix

ADDITIONAL EXERCISES FOR CLASSROOM PRACTICE

1. Select two students to participate in the role-playing situation with the instructor. The roles to be played are as follows:

   Student A—plays the role of the receptionist/operator at Sterling Metal Products Company. All incoming calls are answered at the receptionist/operator's desk before they are transferred to the appropriate person.

   Student B—plays the role of administrative assistant to Mr. John Clement, Director of sales at Sterling Metal Products Company. Mr. Clement is in Europe for two weeks and he has asked his assistant to handle business while he is away.

   Instructor—plays the role of Ms. Dancer, the marketing manager of Teller Stores, a national chain of hardware stores. Ms. Dancer is angry and wishes to speak to Mr. Clement. It seems an order of $250,000 worth of tools has not arrived as scheduled. Teller Stores has already advertised the sale of the tools which is due to begin in a week. She wants specific answers to her questions.

   The other students in the class should watch to see how well the receptionist/operator (Student A) answers the call and transfers Ms. Dancer to the administrative assistant (Student B). They should also evaluate the administrative assistant's handling of the call. Is he/she able to calm down Ms. Dancer and find a solution to the problem? Discussion should follow the exercise to see if techniques discussed in the text have been followed.

Discussion and Evaluation

_____

_____

_____

_____

_____

_____

_____

_____

_____

_____

_____

_____

_____

_____

_____
_____
_____
_____
_____
_____
_____
_____

2. Select two students to participate in the role-playing situation with the instructor. The roles to be played are as follows:

Student A—plays the role of the switchboard operator at Carpenter Fabrics Corporation. All incoming calls are answered at the switchboard before they are transferred to the appropriate person.

Student B—plays the role of the administrative assistant to Howard Como, vice president of the company. Mr. Como has instructed the assistant to screen all calls and to disturb him only if there is something urgent.

Instructor—plays the role of Maureen Belden, a buyer from a national department store chain. Ms. Belden wishes to speak to Mr. Como, and she is hesitant to give out information about herself.

Discussion and Evaluation
_____
_____
_____
_____
_____
_____
_____
_____

3. Select two students to participate in the role-playing situation with the instructor. The roles to be played are as follows:

Student A—plays the role of the switchboard operator at Stearns Advertising. All incoming calls are answered by the switchboard operator before they are transferred to the appropriate person.

Student B—plays the role of administrative assistant to Joan Trent, an account executive who is out of the office. The assistant takes all messages in Ms. Trent's absence. (Takes Mr. Bourne's message.)

```
┌─────────────────────────────────────────┐
│  To _____             │
│                                    A.M.   │
│  Date _____ Time _____   P.M.   │
│                                           │
│          WHILE YOU WERE OUT               │
│                                           │
│  M _____ │
│                                           │
│  of _____ │
│                                           │
│  Phone _____ │
│         Area Code    Number    Extension  │
│                                           │
│  ┌──────────────────┬┬──────────────────┬┐│
│  │ TELEPHONED       ││ PLEASE CALL      ││ │
│  ├──────────────────┼┼──────────────────┼┤│
│  │ CALLED TO SEE YOU││ WILL CALL AGAIN  ││ │
│  ├──────────────────┼┼──────────────────┼┤│
│  │ WANTS TO SEE YOU ││ RUSH             ││ │
│  ├──────────────────┴┴──────────┬───────┘ │
│  │      RETURNED YOUR CALL       │        │
│  └───────────────────────────────┘        │
│                                           │
│  Message _____ │
│  _____│
│  _____│
│  _____│
│                                           │
│                      _____  │
│                              Operator     │
└─────────────────────────────────────────┘
```

Instructor—plays the role of Bill Bourne, a client of Ms. Trent. When Mr. Bourne hears Ms. Trent is not there, he leaves this message: "Tell Joan that Bill Bourne of Acme Publications called. I would like to meet with her next week to discuss a new promotion we are offering. If lunch is okay on Tuesday, that would be perfect. I will call later in the week to confirm. My number is 412-3862."

Discussion and Evaluation

_____

4. Select two students to participate in the role-playing situation with the instructor. The roles to be played are as follows:

Student A—plays the role of the switchboard operator at Webster Investments. All incoming calls are answered at the switchboard before being transferred to the appropriate person.

Student B—plays the role of office assistant to Mr. Leonardo, a financial advisor who has instructed his assistant to screen all calls before connecting. He wants to know the caller's name and the purpose of the call.

Instructor—plays the role of Ward Dewey, a young investor who asks to speak to Mr. Leonardo. Mr. Dewey is planning to open a small account, but he has a number of questions he wants answered first. (Improvise.)

Discussion and Evaluation

_____

_____

_____

_____

_____

_____

_____

_____

_____

_____

_____

_____

_____

5. Select two students to participate in the role-playing situation with the instructor. The roles to be played are as follows:

Student A—plays the role of the switchboard operator at Galvin Travel Services. All incoming calls are answered at the switchboard before being transferred to the appropriate person.

Student B—plays the role of Beth Burke, administrative assistant to Em Galvin, company president. Ms. Galvin is out to lunch and has instructed Ms. Burke to handle any business calls.

Instructor—plays the role of Nancy Tobin, who calls to complain about hotel accommodations in Boston that she and her husband booked as part of a weekend package. Things were so bad, she asks for a refund, which is against company policy. (Improvise.)

ANSWER KEY TO REVIEW QUIZZES

Chapter 1
1. False
2. True
3. False
4. True
5. False
6. True
7. True
8. False
9. False
10. False

Chapter 2
1. True
2. True
3. True
4. False
5. False
6. True
7. True
8. False
9. True
10. True

Chapter 3
1. True
2. True
3. False
4. False
5. True
6. True
7. True
8. False
9. True
10. True

Chapter 4
1. True
2. True
3. False
4. True
5. False
6. True
7. True
8. True
9. False
10. True

Chapter 5
1. True
2. False
3. False
4. True
5. True
6. True
7. True
8. True
9. False
10. True

Chapter 6
1. False
2. True
3. True
4. False
5. True
6. True
7. True
8. True
9. False
10. True

Chapter 7
1. False
2. False
3. True
4. True
5. True
6. True
7. False
8. True
9. True
10. True

To _____

Date _____ Time _____ A.M.
P.M.

WHILE YOU WERE OUT

M _____

of _____

Phone _____
Area Code   Number   Extension

TELEPHONED		PLEASE CALL	
CALLED TO SEE YOU		WILL CALL AGAIN	
WANTS TO SEE YOU		RUSH	
	RETURNED YOUR CALL		

Message _____

_____

_____

_____

_____
Operator

To _____

Date _____   Time _____   A.M.
                                                          P.M.

WHILE YOU WERE OUT

M _____

of _____

Phone _____
            Area Code   Number   Extension

TELEPHONED		PLEASE CALL	
CALLED TO SEE YOU		WILL CALL AGAIN	
WANTS TO SEE YOU		RUSH	
	RETURNED YOUR CALL		

Message _____

_____

_____

_____

                            _____
                                    Operator

To _____

Date _____ Time _____ A.M.
P.M.

WHILE YOU WERE OUT

M _____

of _____

Phone _____

          Area Code   Number   Extension

TELEPHONED		PLEASE CALL	
CALLED TO SEE YOU		WILL CALL AGAIN	
WANTS TO SEE YOU		RUSH	
	RETURNED YOUR CALL		

Message _____

_____

_____

_____

_____
Operator

TELEPHONE VOICE EVALUATION

Speaker: ——————————————

Date: ——————————————

Evaluated by: ——————————————

	WEAK	FAIR	SATISFACTORY	GOOD	VERY GOOD
1. Tone of Voice:					
2. Warmth:					
3. Clarity:					
4. Enthusiasm:					
5. Inflection:					
6. Confidence:					
7. Sincerity:					
8. Volume:					
9. Enunciation:					
10. Pace:					

COMMENTS:

MAJOR STRENGTH(S):

AREAS THAT NEED IMPROVEMENT:

Your instructor may evaluate your voice and/or have your classmates do so. Otherwise, you may tape your own voice and provide your own self-evaluation.

TELEPHONE VOICE EVALUATION

Speaker: ——————————————————

Date: ——————————————————

Evaluated by: ——————————————————

	WEAK	FAIR	SATISFACTORY	GOOD	VERY GOOD
1. Tone of Voice:					
2. Warmth:					
3. Clarity:					
4. Enthusiasm:					
5. Inflection:					
6. Confidence:					
7. Sincerity:					
8. Volume:					
9. Enunciation:					
10. Pace:					

COMMENTS:

MAJOR STRENGTH(S):

AREAS THAT NEED IMPROVEMENT:

Your instructor may evaluate your voice and/or have your classmates do so. Otherwise, you may tape your own voice and provide your own self-evaluation.

TELEPHONE VOICE EVALUATION

Speaker: _____

Date: _____

Evaluated by: _____

	WEAK	FAIR	SATISFACTORY	GOOD	VERY GOOD
1. Tone of Voice:					
2. Warmth:					
3. Clarity:					
4. Enthusiasm:					
5. Inflection:					
6. Confidence:					
7. Sincerity:					
8. Volume:					
9. Enunciation:					
10. Pace:					

COMMENTS:

MAJOR STRENGTH(S):

AREAS THAT NEED IMPROVEMENT:

Your instructor may evaluate your voice and/or have your classmates do so. Otherwise, you may tape your own voice and provide your own self-evaluation.